Collins

D1066696

Real Lives
Real Listening
Elementary A2

Sheila Thorn

Collins

HarperCollins Publishers
77–85 Fulham Palace Road
Hammersmith
London W6 8JB

Originally published in 2009 as three separate titles:
Real Lives, Real Listening: My Family
Real Lives, Real Listening: A Typical Day
Real Lives, Real Listening: A Place I Know Well
by The Listening Business www.thelisteningbusiness.com

Subsequently published by North Star ELT in 2011.

This new edition combining all three titles was published in
2013 by HarperCollins Publishers Ltd

Reprint   10 9 8 7 6 5 4 3 2 1 0

© HarperCollins Publishers Ltd 2013

The right of **Sheila Thorn** to be identified as the Author of this
Work has been asserted by the Publisher in accordance with the
Copyright, Designs and Patents Act 1988.

ISBN 978-0-00-752231-6

Collins® is a registered trademark of HarperCollins Publishers
Limited

www.collinselt.com

A catalogue record of this book is available from the British
Library.

Printed in China by South China Printing Co. Ltd

All images are from Shutterstock. All illustrations are by
Eric Burnett Thorn.

Free teacher's notes and answer keys available online at:
www.collinselt.com

Contents

My Family

Supplementary Units

A Typical Day

A Place I Know Well

Supplementary Units

Teacher's notes and answer keys available online at: **www.collinselt.com**

About the author

The author, Sheila Thorn, is an experienced teacher and materials writer with a particular interest in authentic listening. She is the founder of The Listening Business: www.thelisteningbusiness.com

Acknowledgements

Books, articles, lectures and workshops by the following people have been invaluable in helping me to develop the approach to authentic listening I have used in the *Real Lives, Real Listening* series: Gillian Brown, Ron Carter, Richard Cauldwell, John Field, Jennifer Jenkins, Tony Lynch, Mike McCarthy, Shelagh Rixon, Michael Rost, Paul Seligson, Adrian Underhill, Mary Underwood, Penny Ur and J.J. Wilson.

My grateful thanks to the following people and institutions for commenting on and piloting these materials:

Maria Sforza and Heather Wansbrough-Jones at *South Thames College, London*, Carol Butters, Sarah Dearne, Michelle Parrington and Justin Sales at *Stevenson College, Edinburgh*, Jonathan Fitch at *The Oxford English Centre*, Hazel Black and Chris Jannetta at *English for Everyone, Aberdeen*, Sasha Goldsmith at *Rands English Language Tuition*, Elizabeth Stitt at the *University of St Andrews*, Sophie Freeman, Jen McNair Wilson, John Marquis, Harriet Williams and Jo Whittick at *English in Chester*, Dariana Cristea, Beverley Gray and Keith Harris at *Loughborough College*, Catherine Marshall and Michelle Scolari at *Bellerbys College, London*, Kath Hargreaves, Julia Hudson and Eric Smith at *Embassy CES, Oxford*, Andy Wright at *Queen Mary, University of London*, Zoe Smith at *OISE Bristol*, Elizabeth Bray and Mike Powell at *Coventry College*, Joe Ferrari at *Dundee College* and Julia Isidro at *Kings Oxford*.

I am also extremely grateful to all the people who kindly allowed me to interview them for these books, particularly those for whom English is not their first language.

This book is dedicated to my father and to Jill for their constant love, support and encouragement, and to my late, and greatly missed, mentor Jean Coles.

Introduction

Aims

The main aim of the *Real Lives, Real Listening* series is to provide busy teachers with ready-made listening materials which will effectively *train*, rather than just test, their students in listening. A parallel aim is to boost students' confidence in their listening skills by exposing them to authentic texts. A further aim is to introduce students to the grammatical structures and idiomatic expressions which are typically used in informal spoken English.

The series reflects the latest academic theories on the process of decoding listening input and the importance of authentic listening practice in language acquisition. The series also reflects our new awareness of the huge differences between spoken and written English highlighted by recent research on spoken English corpora.

Authenticity

Unlike the listening texts typically found in coursebooks, each text in *Real Lives, Real Listening* is 100% unscripted. This means that students are exposed to the features of spoken English which they encounter outside the classroom and generally find so daunting. These features include assimilation, elision, linking, weak forms, hesitations, false starts, redundancy and colloquial expressions.

The *Real Lives, Real Listening* series is carefully designed to include both native and near-fluent non-native English speakers, reflecting the fact that most of the English which is spoken these days is between non-native speakers of English.

Content

The series is at three levels: Elementary (A2), Intermediate (B1–B2) and Advanced (B2–C1), with 15 units for each level.

The books are divided into three sections: *My Family*, *A Typical Day* and *A Place I Know Well*. There are five units in each section. The first three contain a wide variety of focused exercises which the teacher can select from, depending on the needs of their students. These units are graded in terms of difficulty, from easier to more challenging. The final two units in each section are for revision purposes. Here the speakers recycle, naturally, the lexis and grammatical structures found in the previous three units. Every unit contains verbatim transcripts of the listening texts and useful glossaries.

Extensive piloting of these materials has shown that students at all levels experience a huge sense of achievement when they find they can actually understand a native or competent non-native speaker talking at a natural speed. The *Real Lives, Real Listening* series provides them with that opportunity.

Sheila M. Thorn

My Family

UNIT 1 Jackie

1. Pre-Listening Comprehension

Jackie comes from Cardiff in South Wales, but she now lives in Cornwall in south-west England. Her accent is a mix of South Welsh and Cornish.

Normalisation – sentence stress

  to

This exercise is designed to help you get used to Jackie's voice.
Listen and underline the stressed words in the following excerpts:

1. I've still got a dad that lives in Cardiff.
2. she's been in hospital as well
3. don't see them as often as we'd like
4. We've got quite a nice life.
5. We can travel a bit.
6. She's been out there for 30 years . . .

A Part 1 – Ticking boxes

Tick (✓) the correct box.

🎧 8

1. Jackie's father is **74** ☐ **48** ☐ **84** ☐.
2. Jackie looks after an elderly **aunt** ☐ **uncle** ☐ **cousin** ☐.
3. Jackie has **two boys** ☐ **two girls** ☐ **a boy and a girl** ☐.
4. Her children work in **Cardiff** ☐ **London** ☐ **Hampshire** ☐.
5. One works for **easyJet.com** ☐ **lastminute.com** ☐ **eBay.com** ☐.
6. Jackie works **part-time** ☐ **full-time** ☐.

B Part 2 – Ticking boxes

Tick (✓) the correct box.

🎧 9

1. Brian likes _____ trees.

   ☐ apple   ☐ fir   ☐ palm

2. He likes plants from _____.

   ☐ Austria   ☐ Australia   ☐ Ostend

3. He builds _____.

   ☐ houses   ☐ planes   ☐ trains

4. Jackie's sister has _____.

   ☐ two boys   ☐ two girls.

A The present simple

Jackie often uses the present simple because she is giving factual information about her family's current situation – things which she sees as permanent. Look at these excerpts:

I now live in Cornwall.
I have an elderly cousin that I look after.
one is married and lives in London
he works in the centre of London
he works for the Audit Office

Note the contrast with the present continuous in this excerpt:

*my younger son lives in Hampshire, but he's now **working** in London*

The meaning here is that he is working in London at the moment, but he wasn't before.

Here are some more examples of the present continuous to talk about things that are happening at the moment:

'<u>I'm calling</u> to ask if you're free tomorrow.'
'Mr Evans <u>is interviewing</u> at the moment. Can he ring you back?'
'<u>We're having</u> a brilliant holiday. I wish you could be here, too.'
'My feet <u>are killing</u> me. Can we stop walking for a bit?'

B *I've got* instead of *I have* in informal spoken English

Notice how Jackie uses *I've got* instead of *I have* for possession. *I've got* is used far more frequently in informal spoken English than in formal spoken English or written English.

I've still got a dad . . .
I've got two sons . . .
When he's got time he builds them.
we've got quite a nice life
she's got two daughters

A Hearing the sounds of English 1

Listen and repeat each minimal pair after the speaker.

live/leave	been/bin
still/steal	hip/heap
look/Luke	side/site

B Discriminating between minimal pairs of sounds 1

Tick (✓) the boxes which correspond to the words you hear.

1	1	2	3	4	5
live					
leave					

2	1	2	3	4	5
still					
steal					

3	1	2	3	4	5
look					
Luke					

4	1	2	3	4	5
been					
bin					

5	1	2	3	4	5
hip					
heap					

6	1	2	3	4	5
side					
site					

C Recognising individual words in a stream of speech 1 – weak forms

Words in informal spoken English often sound very different than the dictionary form. For example, *'from'* changes to *'frum'*, *'been'* changes to *'bin'* and *'to'* changes to *'te'*.

This gap-fill consists of excerpts from the interview and contains words which you should know, but may have problems recognising in a stream of speech.

Before you listen, try to fill in the missing words. Then listen and check your answers.

1. Well, I'm originally _____ Cardiff.
2. I've still got a dad _____ lives in Cardiff.
3. He's 84 _____ we try _____ get up _____ see _____ as much as possible um, especially _____ the moment . . .
4. he's just _____ into hospital _____ a couple _____ weeks, _____ he's out now _____ seems _____ be OK
5. she's _____ in hospital _____ well
6. he works in the centre _____ London
7. working _____ lastminute.com
8. so I've got a prospective daughter-in-law _____ well, which _____ _____ lovely
9. I work part-time _____ the local college, mostly May _____ June . . .
10. he's retired _____ well
11. we _____ travel a bit
12. She's _____ out there _____ 30 years, so I thought, thought it _____ time _____ go!

D Recognising individual words in a stream of speech 2 – linking

When a word ends in a consonant in spoken English and the next word begins with a vowel, the end of the first word will often link with the start of the second word.

Example: I'm_originally from Cardiff. I now live_in Cornwall, which_is a long way from Cardiff.

Mark where you think linking will take place in the following excerpts from the interview, then listen and check your answers.

1. but he's out now and seems to be OK
2. I've still got a dad that lives in Cardiff.
3. I have a, an elderly cousin that I look after . . .
4. she's been in hospital as well
5. one is married and lives in London and he works in the centre of London
6. He likes gardening and er, grows orchids . . .
7. He likes palm trees and er, plants from South Africa and Australia.

E 'er' for pauses

When people are talking they often say 'er' while they are giving themselves time to think about what they are going to say next. This can be confusing because 'er' sounds like 'a'. What sounds do you make in your own language when you are pausing?

Mark where Jackie uses 'er' in the following extracts:

1. and he works in the centre of London dealing with . . .
2. and my younger son lives in Hampshire
3. working for lastminute.com as their marketing and media man
4. No, he's retired as well. He likes gardening and grows orchids.

F **Recognising individual words in a stream of speech 3 – elision**

When speaking quickly in English, people often miss out individual sounds at the ends of words. For example, a speaker will say *las' night* instead of *last night*, *jus' got here* instead of *just got here*, or *trie' to* instead of *tried to.*

Fill in the missing words in these extracts.

1. he's _____ been into hospital for a couple of weeks
2. working for _____.com
3. and the one in Hampshire has now _____ got engaged
4. I _____ part-time at the local college . . .
5. he's gone very exotic in his _____ life down here
6. we've _____ quite a nice life
7. we can travel a bit and _____ to Australia last year
8. It's the _____ time I've ever been out there.

G **Hearing the sounds of English 2**

As with Exercise A, listen and repeat each minimal pair after the speaker.

rest/west	palm/balm
loves/leaves	time/dime
life/live	bit/bid

H Discriminating between minimal pairs of sounds 2

Tick (✓) the boxes which correspond to the words you hear.

1	1	2	3	4	5
rest					
west					
2	1	2	3	4	5
loves					
leaves					
3	1	2	3	4	5
life					
live					
4	1	2	3	4	5
palm					
balm					
5	1	2	3	4	5
time					
dime					
6	1	2	3	4	5
bit					
bid					

I Recognising individual words in a stream of speech 4 – dictation

Work with a partner. Listen to the excerpts from Jackie's interview and write them down. Then check your answers with another pair.

1. _____
2. _____
3. _____
4. _____
5. _____
6. _____
7. _____
8. _____
9. _____
10. _____

J Contractions

Contractions are common in informal spoken and written English, such as two friends chatting, emails between friends, and so on, but not in more formal English such as lectures, speeches and letters to companies.

The following contractions appear in the interview:

he has/he is - *he's*	it is - *it's*
I am - *I'm*	she has - *she's*
I have - *I've*	we have - *we've*

Look at the following excerpts from the interview and put in the appropriate contractions. Then to listen to check your answers.

1. Well, _____ originally from Cardiff . . .
2. _____ still got a dad that lives in Cardiff. _____ 84 . . .
3. Um, _____ been in hospital as well . . .
4. _____ got quite a nice life
5. _____ the first time _____ ever been out there.
6. _____ been out there for 30 years . . .
7. _____ just been into hospital for a couple of weeks
8. on the younger side _____ got two sons
9. _____ now working in London

Cardiff Bay

A Gap–fill

Fill in the blanks with words you heard during Jackie's interview, then listen to check your answers. The missing words are listed in the box to help you.

> daughters   first   from   likes   lives
> time   trees   work   year   years

Interviewer: Does your husband still work?

Jackie: No, he's retired as well. Er, he **(1)** _____ gardening and er, grows orchids and loves . . . he's gone very exotic in his plant life down here. He likes palm **(2)** _____ and er, plants **(3)** _____ South Africa and Australia. And he also likes engines, trains, steam trains and he builds them! When he's, when he's got **(4)** _____ he builds them. But yes, we've got quite a nice life and, as I said, because I **(5)** _____ part-time we can, we can travel a bit and went to Australia last **(6)** _____ to visit my sister who **(7)** _____ out there. And she's got two **(8)** _____, er, so we've had a good time with them and er, seen how she lives. It's the **(9)** _____ time I've ever been out there and she's been out there for 30 **(10)** _____, so I thought, thought it was time to go!

B Extension exercise

Fill in the blanks with words you heard during Jackie's interview. The missing words are listed in the box to help you.

> after   couple   engaged   first   go
> grows   hospital   moment   often   plants
> possible   retired   visit   way   works

1.   The house I live in is a long _____ from the train station.

2.   We try to study as much as _____.

3. I am very happy at the _____.

4. Sam is in _____ with a broken arm.

5. We are going on holiday for a _____ of weeks on 5th September.

6. My son has a cat, but I'm the person who looks _____ it.

7. My grandson _____ in a bank.

8. We don't go the gym as _____ as we'd like.

9. My sister got _____ last week. She's getting married next year.

10. On Sundays we normally _____ friends or relations.

11. My father is _____ now, but he was a teacher for nearly 40 years.

12. My friend _____ tomatoes, potatoes and spinach in her garden.

13. Can you water my _____ for me next week?

14. This is the _____ time I've been to India.

15. I think it's time to _____ – I'm very tired.

C Present simple and present continuous

We looked earlier at Jackie's use of the present simple and continuous.
Put the verbs in brackets into the appropriate tense.

1. We (like) _____ our flat, but (try) _____ to find somewhere bigger so that we can start a family.

2. Thanks for phoning, but I (have) _____ lunch with an old friend from school. Can I call you back?

3. I usually (visit) _____ my grandmother on Sundays, so can we make it another day?

4. My father never (leave) _____ the house without checking that all the windows are shut.

5. I (study) _____ economics this semester, as well as politics and history, so I'm really busy.

6. My best friend (stay) _____ with us for a few days which is really nice.

7. My next-door-neighbour (take) _____ his dog for a walk at seven o'clock every morning, even at the weekend.

D Prepositions and adverbs

Put the correct prepositions or adverbs in these sentences which are based on the interview. Some of them are used more than once.

> at   after   for   from   in   of   on   to   with

1. I know I've got a Birmingham accent now, but I originally come _____ Bristol.
2. Whereabouts _____ London do you live?
3. I'm feeling a bit stressed _____ the moment because of my exams.
4. We're going _____ Greece _____ two weeks at the end _____ August.
5. Could you look _____ my cat while we're away?
6. Have you heard? Anne's _____ hospital with a broken leg!
7. Do you live _____ the centre of Boston?
8. My brother works _____ a company that makes saucepans.
9. I'm starting an art course next week _____ the local college.
10. My parents went _____ Paris _____ for their anniversary.
11. Did you have a good time _____ Daniel on Saturday?

E Transformations

Change the word in each bracket which Jackie used in her interview to form a word which fits the gap.

1. What subject are you (student) _____ at university?
2. What was (live) _____ like in the 1970s?
3. Looking forward to (see) _____ you next week!
4. Could I (possible) _____ have next Friday off?
5. I only wear this necklace on (especially) _____ occasions.
6. I am the (younger) _____ student in the class by three days.
7. What's the (mostly) _____ you've ever paid for a holiday?
8. Everyone in my class is very (friends) _____.
9. What's that big (builds) _____ over there? It looks like a theatre.
10. Because we live near the sea we get lots of (visit) _____ in the summer.

I: Can you tell me something about your family – your parents, your grandparents, cousins, aunts, uncles, children?

J: Right, right. Well, **(1) I'm originally from Cardiff**. I now live in **(2) Cornwall**, which is a long way from Cardiff. I've still got a dad that lives in Cardiff. He's 84 and we try and get up and see him as much as possible um, especially at the moment when he's, he's just been into hospital for a couple of weeks but he's out now and seems to be OK. Um, down here I have a, an elderly cousin that I look after. Um, she's been in hospital as well – with a fractured, **(3) a fractured hip**, but she's come out now and **(4) she seems to be coping** well as well. Er, on the younger side I've got two sons, er, both . . . one, one is married and lives in London and he works in the centre of London er, **(5) dealing with** . . . he works for the Audit Office dealing with er, at the moment East, Eastern European countries. And my younger son er, lives in **(6) Hampshire**, but he's now working in London and . . . can I say the company? Er, work, working for lastminute.com er, as their **(7) marketing and media man**. Er, we don't see them as often as we'd like but er, the one in, er, in London, who lives in London is, is married, so I've got, I've got **(8) a daughter-in-law**, and the one in Hampshire **(9) has now just got engaged**, so I've got a **(10) prospective** daughter-in-law as well, which will be lovely. Er, my husband and I er, are both . . . I, I work part-time at the local college, mostly May and June, so the rest of the year I travel and visit friends and relations.

I: Does your husband still work?

J: No, he's retired as well. Er, he likes gardening and er, grows **(11) orchids** and loves . . . he's gone very **(12) exotic** in his plant life down here. He likes palm trees and er, plants from South Africa and Australia. And he also likes engines, trains, steam trains and he builds them! When he's, when he's got time he builds them. But yes, we've got quite a nice life and, as I said, because I work part-time we can, we can travel a bit and went to Australia last year to visit my sister who lives out there. And she's got two daughters er, so we've had a good time with them and er, seen how she lives. It's the first time I've ever been out there and she's been out there for 30 years, so I thought, thought it was time to go!

1   **I'm originally from Cardiff.** – Jackie was born in Cardiff, but she moved away. Cardiff is the capital of Wales and is a large port.
2   Cornwall – the most south-westerly county in England
3   **a fractured hip** – The adjective 'fractured' means broken. The hip is the joint which connects the leg to the upper part of the body.
4   **she seems to be coping well** – she appears to be managing well, despite her fractured hip
5   **dealing with** – working with
6   Hampshire – a county in the middle of the south coast of England, between the counties of Dorset and West Sussex
7   **(a) marketing and media man** – the man responsible for trying to get new customers whose job involves dealing with advertising in newspapers and on television
8   **a daughter-in-law** – the woman who is married to your son
9   **has now just got engaged** – has just announced formally that he and his girlfriend have decided they are going to get married
10 prospective – future
11 orchids (plural) – interestingly shaped and colourful flowers often found in rainforests
12 exotic – very unusual because they come from distant countries

UNIT 2 Micky

1. Pre-Listening Comprehension

Micky has lived and worked in east London for most of his life and he has a strong east London accent. For many years he worked as a legal executive, but he currently runs a pub in Walthamstow, east London. He has been married twice, divorced once and he now lives with his partner, Carole.

A Normalisation – recognising features of a London accent

People with a London accent often:

1. leave the final −d off the word *and*, as in these examples:

   'Tammy an' Tiffany'
   'one, an' one on the way'
   'She has er, two brothers an' two sisters.'

2. use a glottal stop with the word *got*. The glottal stop is a common feature of many British accents. The glottal stop occurs when the speaker constricts his or her throat and blocks the air stream completely. This results in the speaker not pronouncing fully the −t sound at the end of words such as *got* or *lot*, or the −t− sounds in words such as *bottle* or *kettle*.

   'Tammy's <u>got</u> two. Tiffany's <u>got</u> one . . .'

B Normalisation – anticipating the next word

Listen to tracks 34–38. There is a word missing from the end of each excerpt. Try to guess the missing word and write it down. Then listen to tracks 39–43 to check your answers. How well did you guess?

1. _____
2. _____
3. _____
4. _____
5. _____

Corrections

Listen and correct the mistake in each sentence.

1. There are five years between Tammy and Tiffany.
2. Nathalie, Danny and Michelle are all in their 20s.
3. The oldest three children all have the same mother.
4. Micky has four children altogether.
5. Tammy and Tiffany have both got one child.
6. Micky has been married three times.
7. Micky's partner Carole is in her 30s.
8. Carole works in a shop.
9. Thomas is older than James.
10. Carole has got five brothers and sisters.
11. One of Carole's sisters lives in England.

A Present simple and present continuous

Micky uses the present simple in these excerpts because he is describing what he views as a permanent situation.

> *And she works with me in the pub.*
> *The others all live in Ireland.*

Note the contrast with the present continuous in these excerpts from the interview where Micky and the interviewer are talking about the situation at the moment.

> *Michelle is expecting.*
> *And you're just waiting . . .*

B *I've got* instead of *I have* in informal spoken English

As with Jackie in Unit 1, notice how often the interviewer uses *have got* instead of *have* for possession.

> *So you've got five children?*
> *Have you got any grandchildren?*
> *Have you got a partner at the moment?*
> *Has she got children?*
> *Have you got any uncles and aunties?*

A Falling intonation for statements

When we make a statement in English our voice falls at the end of the statement. This also indicates that the speaker has finished talking. Listen to Micky making the following statements and mark where his voice begins to fall, as in the first example.

1. She is 44 years of age.
2. She has er, three children.
3. I don't know her age.
4. She has er, two brothers and two sisters.
5. The others all live in Ireland.

Now write three sentences about yourself and read them out with the correct intonation. For example:

My name is Yasmin.   I am 25 years old.   I live in Bristol.

B Recognising individual words in a stream of speech 1– linking

When a word ends in a consonant in spoken English and the next word begins with a vowel, the end of the first word will often link with the start of the second word.

Example: So . . . what are their names_again?

Mark where you think linking will take place in the following excerpts from the interview, then listen and check your answers.

1. So five altogether.
2. she is 44 years of age
3. Her eldest is Kim.
4. Have you got any uncles and aunties?
5. Has Carole got any brothers and sisters?
6. one is in England
7. The others all live in Ireland.

C Hearing the sounds of English 1

Listen and repeat each minimal pair after the speaker.

three/free	uncles/ankles
time/Tim	works/walks
think/sink	

D Discriminating between minimal pairs of sounds 1

Listen and underline the words you hear.

1. They are all **three/free**.
2. It's **time/Tim**!
3. I can't **think/sink** now.
4. Look at your **uncles/ankles**!
5. She **works/walks** very fast.

E Recognising individual words in a stream of speech 2 – gap-fill

It is sometimes difficult to hear individual words in a stream of speech. Try to guess the missing words in these extracts, then listen to check your answers and fill in any words you couldn't guess.

1. I have er, a daughter _____ Tammy.
2. So you've _____ five children?
3. The first two, the _____ two, with _____ first wife.
4. the other three _____ are from my _____ marriage
5. Have you got _____ grandchildren?
6. Have you got a _____ at the moment?
7. I _____ know her age.
8. If I _____ I don't know _____ they are.
9. The others _____ live in Ireland.

F 'er' for pauses

When people are talking they often say *'er'* while they are giving themselves time to think about what they are going to say next. This can be confusing because *'er'* sounds like *'a'*. What sounds do you make in your own languages when you are pausing?

Listen to the following excerpts and mark where Micky uses *'er'*.

1. I have a daughter called Tammy.
2. Her name is Carole and she is 44 years of age.
3. She has three children.
4. She has two brothers and two sisters.

G Sentence stress

Stressed words are the most important in spoken English because they carry the most meaning.

Mark which words you think will be stressed in the following excerpts and then listen and check their answers.

1. The first two, the oldest two, with my first wife.
2. the other three children are from my second marriage
3. Tammy's got two.
4. Her name is Carole and er, she is 44 years of age.
5. She has er, three children. Her eldest is Kim.
6. Her mum is alive.
7. The others all live in Ireland.

H Hearing the sounds of English 2

As with Exercise C, listen and repeat each minimal pair after the speaker.

called/cold	is/his
first/thirst	alive/arrive
years/jeers	live/life

| | Discriminating between minimal pairs of sounds 2

Tick (✓) the boxes which correspond to the words you hear.

1	1	2	3	4	5
called					
cold					

2	1	2	3	4	5
first					
thirst					

3	1	2	3	4	5
years					
jeers					

4	1	2	3	4	5
is					
his					

5	1	2	3	4	5
alive					
arrive					

6	1	2	3	4	5
live					
life					

J Recognising individual words in a stream of speech 3 – weak forms

The dictionary form of prepositions changes to a weaker form in spoken English which is not as clear.

Listen and fill in the missing prepositions. Some of them are used more than once.

for	from	in	of	on	with

1. Starting _____ children?
2. The first two, the oldest two, _____ my first wife.
3. the other three children are _____ my second marriage
4. Three, _____ two _____ their way.
5. Divorced once, pending now _____ the second time.
6. She works _____ me _____ the pub.
7. One is _____ England . . . one _____ her brothers.

K Recognising individual words in a stream of speech 4 – elision

When speaking quickly in English, people often miss out individual sounds at the ends of words. For example, a speaker will say *las' night* instead of *last night*, *jus' got here* instead of *just got here*, or *trie' to* instead of *tried to*.

Fill in the missing words in these extracts.

1. I have er, a daughter _____ Tammy aged 34 . . .
2. Interviewer: All with the same wife?

   Micky: No. The _____ two, the _____ two, with my _____ wife.
3. the other three children are from my _____ marriage
4. Have you got any _____?
5. Um, so you've been _____ twice.
6. _____ you're _____ waiting . . .

5. Further Language Development

A Extension exercise

Fill in the blanks with words you heard during Micky's interview.

> alive   any   daughter   expecting   grandchildren
> marriage   married   partner   wife   works

1. Suki has two sons and one _____.
2. I met my _____ at a party. We got married nine years ago.
3. A lot of young people don't believe in _____. They live with their partners instead.
4. I have six _____. My daughter has two boys and my son has three girls and a boy.
5. My sister is _____ a baby next March.
6. I've been _____ for three years.
7. My _____ and I are getting married next year.
8. My oldest brother _____ in my father's restaurant.
9. My mother's father is still _____, but her mother died in 1995.
10. Have you got _____ children yourself?

B Personal pronouns into possessive pronouns

Change the personal pronoun in the bracket into the corresponding possessive pronoun.

1. Where did you park (you) _____ car?
2. Have you met (I) _____ brother Simon?
3. Did your parents enjoy (they) _____ holiday?
4. Do you like (we) _____ new carpet?
5. My son can't stop talking about (he) _____ new girlfriend.
6. My sister met (she) _____ husband at university.
7. The cat has got (it) _____ own bed in the kitchen.

C Cardinal numbers into ordinal numbers

Micky talks about his first wife and his second marriage. Put the numbers in the brackets into their correct form.

1. This is the (3) _____ time he's rung me today.
2. This is the (4) _____ time we've been to Portugal on holiday.
3. This is the (5) _____ day it's rained in a row.
4. Turn into Somers Road and we're the (6) _____ house on the right.
5. What's the date today? Is it the (7) _____ or the (8) _____?
6. Isn't *i* the (9) _____ letter of the alphabet?
7. We're having a party on the (10) _____. Can you make it?

D does, doesn't and don't

Put *does*, *doesn't* or *don't* in the gaps, where appropriate.

1. We _____ normally eat white bread.
2. I'm sure Peter _____ like dogs, so we'll have to put Spot in the garden when he gets here.
3. What _____ your mother work as?
4. Who _____ the cooking? You or your husband?
5. Why _____ we meet up for a coffee sometime?
6. My brother _____ say much because he's quite shy.
7. What time _____ your train leave?
8. You _____ look very well. Are you OK?
9. My suit _____ fit me any more. I must go on a diet.
10. Why _____ Peter's parents eat potatoes?

I: Can you tell me about your family please, Mick?
M: Yes. Starting with children?
I: Yeah.
M: Yes. I have er, a daughter called Tammy aged 34, Tiffany, 31, Nathalie, 24, Danny, 21 and Michelle, 19.
I: So you've got five children?
M: Yes.
I: All with the same wife?
M: No. The first two, the oldest two, with my first wife.
I: So . . . what are their names again?
M: That's Tammy and Tiffany.
I: OK. So with your first wife.
M: My first wife, marriage, and the other three children are from my second marriage.
I: OK. Right. So five altogether. Have you got any grandchildren?
M: Three, (1) **with two on their way.**
I: Really! (*laughs*) So which of the children have had children?
M: Tammy's got two.
I: Right.
M: Tiffany's got one, and one on the way, and (2) **Michelle is expecting.**
I: (3) **Goodness me!** OK. Um, so you've been married twice.
M: Yes.
I: Divorced twice?
M: Divorced once, (4) **pending** now for the second time.
I: OK. So (5) **you've applied for a divorce?**
M: Yes.
I: And you're just waiting . . .

M: Yes.
I: Right. Have you got (6) **a partner** at the moment?
M: Yes.
I: Can you tell me about her?
M: I can. Her name is Carole and er, she is 44 years of age. And she works with me (7) **in the pub.**
I: OK . . .
M: . . . in (8) **Walthamstow.**
I: Has she got children?
M: She has er, three children. Her eldest is Kim. I don't know her age, but I think 24, James who is 19 and Thomas who is 14.
I: Right. Um, are your mum and dad alive?
M: No.
I: No. OK. Um, what about Carole's mum and dad?
M: Her mum is alive. Her father's er, (9) **deceased,** some time back.
I: OK. Have you got any uncles and aunties?
M: No.
I: No. Have you got any cousins?
M: Er, hmm, if I have I don't know where they are.
I: OK. (*laughs*) Has Carole got any brothers and sisters?
M: She has er, two brothers and two sisters.
I: Right. Are they all in England?
M: Er, one is in England . . . one of her brothers. The others all live in Ireland.
I: OK. (10) **Whereabouts?**
M: (11) **Round about the Dublin area.**
I: OK.

1   **with two on their way** – two more grandchildren who haven't been born yet
2   **Michelle is expecting** – Michelle is going to have a baby.
3   **Goodness me!** – The interviewer is very surprised.
4   **pending** – a legal term meaning 'waiting to happen'
5   **you've applied for a divorce** – you have officially requested a divorce
6   **a partner** – a person who you live with or are married to
7   **in the pub** – A pub is a bar where you can drink alcoholic and non-alcoholic drinks and where people go to relax and meet friends.
8   **Walthamstow** – an area of north-east London
9   **deceased** – a legal term meaning 'dead'
10 **Whereabouts?** – In what part (of a country, city, etc.)?
11 **Round about the Dublin area.** – in and around Dublin

UNIT **3** Tammy

A Discussion

Tammy grew up in Canada but left in her 20s. She now works as a theatre sister and lives in east London, but she has retained her Canadian accent.

1. What do you think of when you hear the word 'Canada'?
2. How much do you know about Canada?
3. Have you been to Canada?
4. Would you like to go to Canada? Why? / Why not?
5. Do you know what a Canadian accent sounds like in your own language?

B Normalisation –
gap-fill

This exercise is designed to help you get used to Tammy's voice.
Listen and fill in the missing information.

Registration Form

Name: **Tammy St.** _____

Address: _____ **Road, London**

Postcode: _____

Telephone number: (work) _____

(mobile) _____

Date of Birth: _____

A Multiple choice

Tammy talks about her parents and grandparents. Underline the correct answers.

1. Tammy's mother was born in Scotland/Canada/Germany.
2. Tammy's grandfather had to leave Prussia/Persia/Russia.
3. Tammy was born in Canada/Germany.
4. Tammy's father was in the British Army/German Army/Canadian Army.

B Note-taking

Tammy talks about her brother, Stephen and her sister, Susan. Fill in the notes.

Stephen

1. Age: _____
2. Married/Single: _____
3. Number of children: _____
4. Lives in: _____
5. Job: _____

Susan

6. Lives in: _____
7. Number of children: _____

C Gap-fill

Tammy talks about her sister and her two other brothers. Listen and fill in the missing words.

Before you listen, try to predict which words, or which **types** of words (nouns, adjectives, prepositions, parts of verbs, etc.) will fit in the gaps. Then listen and check your answers.

1. Tammy's second-oldest sister Nancy is married to _____ and lives in Whistler.
2. Tammy's brother Brian has three _____.
3. The oldest child is going to start _____ soon.
4. Tammy's brother Bruce has two little _____.
5. Bruce and his wife recently bought a _____ for the first time.

D Questions

Tammy talks about Whistler, a famous ski resort north of Vancouver. Listen and answer the questions.

1. Which word does Tammy use to describe Whistler?
2. Why didn't Tammy go to Whistler the last time she was in Canada?
3. How does Tammy normally travel to Whistler?
4. Has the interviewer ever been to Whistler?

A The present simple

We generally use the present simple when we are talking about situations which we see as permanent. Look at these examples from the interview:

> they <u>live</u> up at Whistler and they <u>don't have</u> kids between the two of them . . . they <u>have</u> a nice life up there
> three of them <u>live</u> in Edmonton and then Stephen <u>lives</u> in Ontario and Nancy <u>lives</u> in Whistler.
> I <u>go</u> up there whenever I <u>can</u> 'cos my sister <u>lives</u> there.
> Jill's sister <u>works</u> on that train.

B Forming questions using *do/does* and *did*

To form a question in the present simple we use *do/does* + subject + verb. Tammy says her mum's parents both came from Germany. The interviewer says:

> <u>Do you know</u> where in Germany?

If we are asking a question in the third person (he/she/it) we use *does*, as in these examples:

> 'Where <u>does he live</u>?'
> 'What time <u>does she finish</u>?'
> 'How <u>does it look</u>?'

To form a question in the simple past we use *did* + verb. When asking about Tammy's parents, the interviewer says:

> <u>did they</u> originally <u>come</u> from Scotland, or . . .?

Tammy says she was born in Germany. The interviewer says:

> How <u>did that happen</u>?

C Introduction to the present perfect simple

We use the present perfect simple to talk about things which have (or haven't) happened during a period of time leading up to the present. To form the present perfect simple we use the verb ***have*** + past participle.

1. The present perfect simple with ***just***

We often use the present perfect simple with *just* to talk about things that have happened very recently. The word *just* fits between *has/have* and the past participle, as in these examples:

'I <u>have just heard</u> I have passed my exam!'
'<u>We have just come back</u> from holiday, so we are a bit tired.'
'Pierre <u>has just left</u>.'

We often shorten *has/have* in spoken English to *'s* or *'ve*:

'<u>I've</u> just heard <u>I've</u> passed my exam!'
'<u>We've</u> just come back from holiday, so we are a bit tired.'
'<u>Pierre's just left</u>.'

Now look at these examples from the interview. When talking about her brother Brian's children, Tammy says:

His oldest <u>one's just graduated</u> from high school.

When talking about her youngest brother Bruce and his wife, Tammy says:

<u>*they've just bought*</u> *their first house*

2. The present perfect simple with questions and answers:

Interviewer: *<u>Have you been</u> up there a lot?*

Tammy: *<u>I've been</u> up there a few times.*

Interviewer: *<u>Have you ever taken</u> that train from Vancouver to Whistler?*

Tammy: *No, <u>I've never done</u> that. <u>I've always just driven up</u>.*

D Expressing surprise

We often use a rise and a fall (⟋ ⟍) to express surprise. Look at these examples from the interview:

Tammy: *But my mum's parents were both from Germany.*
Interviewer: *Oh, really?*
Tammy: *Well, I was actually born there.*
Interviewer: *Were you?*
Tammy: *I have five brothers and sisters.*
Interviewer: *Really?*

Now practise making statements and expressing surprise.

A **Recognising individual words in a stream of speech**

Work with a partner. Listen to the excerpts from Tammy's interview and write them down. Then check your answers with another pair.

1. _____.

2. _____

3. _____?

4. _____.

5. _____.

6. _____.

B **Hearing the sounds of English 1**

Listen and repeat each minimal pair after the speaker.

they/day	lives/leaves
had/hat	try/dry
fairly/fairy	

C **Discriminating between minimal pairs of sounds 1**

Tick (✓) the boxes which correspond to the words you hear.

1	1	2	3	4	5
they					
day					
2	1	2	3	4	5
had					
hat					
3	1	2	3	4	5
fairly					
fairy					
4	1	2	3	4	5
lives					
leaves					
5	1	2	3	4	5
try					
dry					

D Contractions

Contractions are common in informal spoken and written English, such as two friends chatting, emails between friends, and so on, but not in more formal English such as lectures, speeches and letters to companies.

With a partner, practise saying the contracted forms of these phrases in pairs.

did not	do not	He is	I am	I have	one is
that is	there is	they are	they have	who is	

Now look at the following excerpts from the interview and put in the appropriate contractions. Then listen to check your answers.

Example: And (I am) <u>I'm</u> not sure how my grandmother got to Canada either.

1. And (that is) _____ why we ended up in Chilliwack . . .
2. (He is) _____ married with one child.
3. And then (I have) _____ got another sister . . .
4. they (do not) _____ have kids between the two of them
5. then (there is) _____ Brian — married, three kids
6. His oldest (one has) _____ just graduated from high school . . .
7. and (they have) _____ just bought their first house which (they are) _____ rather excited about
8. (I have) _____ been there a few times.
9. I (did not) _____ make it last time . . .

E Hearing the sounds of English 2

As with Exercise B, listen and repeat each minimal pair after the speaker.

other/udder	high/eye
bid/bit	spend/spent
fifty/fifteen	

F **Discriminating between minimal pairs of sounds 2**

Tick (✓) the boxes which correspond to the words you hear.

1	1	2	3	4	5
other					
udder					
2	1	2	3	4	5
bid					
bit					
3	1	2	3	4	5
fifty					
fifteen					
4	1	2	3	4	5
high					
eye					
5	1	2	3	4	5
spend					
spent					

G **Linking**

Linking occurs when the end of one word **runs_into** the **start_of** the next word. It is very common in informal spoken English, but less so in more formal English, such as speeches or lectures.

The most common linking occurs between the letter *–s* at the end of a word when the next word begins with a vowel, as in these excerpts from the interview:

> *He was_at Moscow University . . .*
> *dad was_in the army*

However, linking also occurs with other sounds, as in these excerpts from the interview:

> *they spent_a lot of time in_an_Indian village*
> *Yeah, that's_what she was_saying.*
> *Yeah, you guys_should try it.*

Mark where you think linking occurs in these excerpts from the interview, then listen and check your answers.

1. Well, I was actually born there.
2. He was an engineer . . .
3. I have five brothers and sisters.
4. He lives in Ontario.
5. He's a great guy.
6. she's a stepmom to his kid

H Hearing the sounds of English 3

As with Exercises B and E, listen and repeat each minimal pair after the speaker.

either/ether   kid/kit
began/begun   gorgeous/gorges
there/dare

I Discriminating between minimal pairs of sounds 3

Tick (✓) the boxes which correspond to the words you hear.

1	1	2	3	4	5
either					
ether					
2	1	2	3	4	5
began					
begun					
3	1	2	3	4	5
there					
dare					
4	1	2	3	4	5
kid					
kit					
5	1	2	3	4	5
gorgeous					
gorges					

J Simplification - elision

When speaking quickly in English, people often miss out individual sounds at the ends of words. For example, a speaker will say *las' night* instead of *last night*, *jus' got here* instead of *just got here*, or *trie' to* instead of *tried to*.

Fill in the missing words in these extracts.

1. And I'm not sure how my grandmother _____ _____ Canada either.
2. My sister _____ _____ lives in Ed . . . Alberta.
3. He's a _____ _____.
4. And then I've got another sister who's er, _____ _____ Tony . . .
5. and my _____ _____ Bruce
6. His oldest one's _____ _____ from high school . . .
7. they've _____ _____ their first house
8. I didn't make it _____ _____ 'cos of mum being in hospital . . .
9. I've always _____ _____ up.

K Simplification – weak forms

Words in informal spoken English often sound very different than the dictionary form. For example, *'from'* changes to *'frum'*, *'been'* changes to *'bin'* and 'to' changes to *'te'*.

This gap-fill consists of excerpts from the interview and contains words which you should know, but may have problems recognising in a stream of speech. Before you listen, try to fill in the missing words. Then listen and check your answers.

1. Um, your parents, did they originally come _____ Scotland, or . . .?
2. They were both born _____ Ontario . . .
3. He was _____ Moscow University when all the troubles began . . .
4. dad was _____ the army
5. He's married _____ one child.
6. **and** they spent a lot _____ time _____ an Indian village
7. And then I've got another sister who's er, married _____ Tony.
8. His oldest one's just graduated _____ high school, starting college . . .
9. and they've just bought their first house, which they're rather excited _____
10. I didn't make it last time 'cos, 'cos of mum being _____ hospital . . .

A Extension exercise Fill in the blanks in these new sentences with words you heard during Tammy's interview. The words are listed in the box to help you.

> born   bought   child   does   excited   gorgeous
> got   graduate   great   hospital   just   lot
> make   married   oldest   originally   out
> parents   should   spent   train   village

1. My _____ moved to a mobile home once we'd all left home.

2. Los Cristianos was _____ a little fishing village, but now it's a major tourist resort.

3. I was _____ on Christmas Day as well!

4. We got _____ at the wrong station, so we had to buy another ticket.

5. What _____ your wife work as?

6. Katie's the youngest student and Petra is the _____.

7. Stefan and Carla are getting _____ next year.

8. We _____ so much money on holiday! We've never been anywhere so expensive before.

9. I used to get a _____ of headaches when I was a _____.

10. We live in a small _____ of about 2,000 inhabitants.

11. We had a _____ time on holiday. You should have come with us!

12. I'm going to have huge party when I _____ from university.

13. Sarah _____ me a new top for my birthday. Isn't it wonderful?

14. I'm really _____ about my new job.

15. This lasagne is _____! Would you like to try some?

16. We're having a barbecue next Saturday. Can you _____ it?

17. Christoph's in _____ with a broken leg so I'm going to visit him later.

18. When we were in Norway we took a _____ from Oslo to Bergen.

19. Don't worry about cooking us dinner. We'll _____ have a sandwich.

20. You've _____ a terrible cough. You _____ go to the doctor.

B Questions with do/does and did

Form questions from the words in brackets, using *do*, *does* or *did*.
Look at the examples first:

You (cook) dinner every night?	**Do you cook dinner every night?**
He (take) sugar?	**Does he take sugar?**
You (have) a good holiday?	**Did you have a good holiday?**

1. you (like) swimming?

   _____

2. you (close) the window before we left?

   _____

3. you (enjoy) the party last night?

   _____

4. it (rain) a lot in Boston?

   _____

5. you ever (have) to work late?

   _____

6. this train (go) to Wigan?

   _____

7. you (study) Latin when you were at school?

   _____

8. you (want) to stop now for a cup of coffee?

   _____

9. she (like) the present you got her for her birthday?

   _____

10. your garden (get) a lot of sun?

    _____

11. you (know) if Martin passed his driving test?

    _____

12. your teacher (give) you a lot of homework?

    _____

C Transformations

Change each word in brackets taken from the interview to make them fit the gap.

1. It's Alain's (birth) _____ on Saturday, so don't forget to send him a card.

2. Thanks for lending me that book. It was very (interested) _____.

3. My sister Caroline is two years (oldest) _____ than me.

4. Sarah loves (child) _____ so she's going to train to be a (teaching) _____.

5. We used to (life) _____ in Boston, but we moved to Vermont when we had the kids.

6. We're going to (bought) _____ a new car next week.

7. This book is so (excited) _____! You must read it!

8. We (taken) _____ our kids to the circus last week and they loved it.

9. Do you like (driven) _____?

10. I (works) _____ through my lunch break so I'm starving! What's for dinner?

Part 1: Personal Details   (54")

I: Um, if I could just start with some **(1) personal details.** Can I have your name, please?

T: It's Tammy St. John.

I: OK. How do you um, do the St. John? Is that two separate words?

T: It's er, S-T **(2) dot** John.

I: OK. And your address.

T: It's er, 313a Hainault Road.

I: Hainault. How do you spell that?

T: H-A-I-N-A-U-L-T.

I: OK and er, that's London?

T: Yes.

I: Yeah. And the postcode?

T: N11 1ES.

I: OK. And your daytime telephone number.

T: 0208 550 3451.

I: OK. And do you have a mobile?

T: Yes.

I: Can I have that number?

T: You want that one as well.

I: Yes please. **(3) It's just for** our files.

T: OK. 07742 135211.

I: OK. And your date of birth.

T: 9th of the 12th, '61.

I: OK. Thanks very much.

Part 2: My Family   (2'47")

I: Um, your parents, **(4) did they originally come from Scotland,** or . . .?

T: No.

I: No?

T: Not even from Canada. (*laughs*) Well, they did. They were both born in Ontario, but my mum's parents were both from Germany.

I: Oh, really?

T: Yes.

I: Do you know where in Germany?

T: Not really, no. Um, I know my grandfather was **(5) Prussian,** I think. **(6) He was at Moscow University** when all the troubles began and he had to get out 'cos of . . . the family he was in or whatever. And I'm not sure how my grandmother got to Canada either. But they were from **(7) a fairly wealthy family** there as well, but . . . they all got out.

I: Have you been interested to go to Germany and try and track them down — **(8) track down your family?**

T: **(9) Well, I was actually born there.**

I: Were you?

T: Yeah. (*laughs*)

I: How did that happen?

T: Army.

I: Your . . . dad.

T: Dad. Yeah, dad was in **(10) the army. (11) The only foreign-born kid.**

I: Right. Um, what was his work?

T: He was **(12) an engineer, Royal Engineer.**

I: OK.

T: **(13) Sergeant. (14) And that's why we ended up in** Chilliwack 'cos there was **(15) an engineering army base** there.

I: So Canadian Army.

T: Yes. Yes.

I: Right. OK. You . . . Er, you've got brothers and sisters there.

T: I have five brothers and sisters.

I: Really?! (*laughs*)

T: Yeah! (*laughs*)

I: Can we go through them?

T: If you like. We start with the oldest, is Stephen. He's er, 50 now. He's married with one child. He lives in Ontario. Er, they spent a lot of time in an Indian village teaching children for years after they got **(16) their er, teaching credentials.** Um, I have another sister called Susan. My sister called Susan lives in Ed . . . Alberta. Married, one kid who's . . . he's 25 or 26 now. **(17) He's a great guy.** He's turned out really well. And then I've got another sister who's er, married to Tony, and they live up at Whistler and they don't have kids between the two of them, but she's **(18) a stepmom** to his kid and, um, and they have a nice life up there. Er, then there's Brian — married, three kids. Nice kids. **(19) His oldest one's just graduated from high school,** starting college. And the other one, the next one'll graduate next year. Um, and my youngest brother Bruce, he's married with two little girls and they've just bought their first house, which they're rather excited about. And again he lives in Edmonton as well as Brian. So they're all, **(20) spread out a bit.**

I: They are, aren't they?

T: Well, three of them live in Edmonton and then Stephen lives in Ontario and Nancy lives in Whistler.

I: OK. **(21) Whistler's supposed to be absolutely beautiful.**

T:	(22) It's gorgeous.		T:	No, I've never done that. I've always just driven up.
I:	Have you been there a lot?		I:	OK. 'Cos um, Jill's sister works on that train.
T:	I've been there a few times. (23) I didn't make it last		T:	Yeah, that's what she was saying.
	time 'cos, 'cos of mum being in hospital, but yeah, I go up		I:	It sounds wonderful.
	there whenever I can 'cos my sister lives there. So . . .		T:	Yeah, you guys should try it.
I:	Have you ever taken that train from Vancouver up to		I:	(24) Yep, one day.
	Whistler?		T:	Yep.

7. Words and Phrases

1   **personal details** (plural) – personal information: name, address, date of birth, etc.
2   **dot** – a very small round mark (in this case a full stop)
3   **It's just for our files.** – It's just for our records, i.e. the information we keep about people.
4   **did they originally come from Scotland** – Were they born in Scotland?
5   **Prussian** – coming from Prussia (Prussia no longer exists, but historically Prussia was the dominant state in northern Germany and its capital was Berlin.)
6   **He was at Moscow University when all the troubles began** – He was at Moscow University when the First World War broke out in 1914 and Russia and Germany became enemies.
7   **a fairly wealthy family** – quite a rich family
8   **track down your family** – try to find out information about your family
9   **Well, I was actually born there.** – Well, in fact I was born there.
10   **the army** – Canada's military force, which is now part of the Canadian Forces
11   **The only foreign-born kid.** – The only child who was born abroad. (*kid* is a slang word for *child*.)
12   **an engineer, Royal Engineer** – a soldier working with machines in the Canadian Army, now known as the Canadian Forces
13   **(a) Sergeant.** – A sergeant is a middle-ranking soldier.
14   **And that's why we ended up in Chilliwack** – And that's how we came to live in Chilliwack
15   **an engineering army base** – a place with military buildings where members of the army live
16   **their er, teaching credentials** (plural) – their teaching qualifications
17   **He's a great guy.** – He's a really nice man. (*guy* is a slang word for *man*)
18   **a stepmom** – (AmE) (BrE **stepmum**) – a woman who is married to, or living with the child's father, but who is not the child's birth mother
19   **His oldest one's just graduated from high school** – His oldest child has just finished his secondary education.
20   **spread out a bit** – they live in different places covering a large area
21   **Whistler's supposed to be absolutely beautiful.** – People say Whistler is very beautiful.
22   **It's gorgeous.** – It's very beautiful.
23   **I didn't make it last time** – I didn't manage to get there last time.
24   **yep** – yes. (informal)

UNIT 4 Anne-Maj

Anne-Maj lives in Sweden. She speaks good English and visits London regularly, but she has a strong Swedish accent.

Normalisation

Anne-Maj talks about her children and grandchildren. This exercise is designed to help you get used to Anne-Maj's voice. Listen and fill in the missing words.

1. Anne-Maj comes from _____ Sweden.
2. She lives in a town called _____.
3. She has _____ daughters.
4. Annette is _____, Marie will be _____ in September and Camilla is _____.
5. Anne-Maj has _____ grandchildren — _____ girls and _____ boys.
6. Her oldest grandson will be _____ in _____ and her youngest grandchild is _____.

A Gap-fill 1

86

Listen and fill in the missing words.

1. Anne-Maj talks about her grandchildren. She gives her grandchildren's names from the youngest to the oldest. Fill in the missing names: Erika, Hannah, _____, Magnus, Marcus, Patrik, Mathias and _____.

2. Anne-Maj's oldest grandson got his own _____ a month ago.

3. He's got a girlfriend, but he is planning to live on his _____ at least for now.

B Questions

87

Anne-Maj talks about her brothers and sisters. Answer the questions.

1. How many brothers and sisters does Anne-Maj have?
2. How old is Anne-Maj's oldest brother?
3. How old is her youngest brother?
4. How far is the town where Anne-Maj was born from the town where she lives in now?
5. What is the name of the town Anne-Maj comes from originally?

C Gap-fill 2

88

Anne-Maj talks about her husband Arne's children from his previous marriage. Listen and fill in the missing words.

1. Arne has _____ girls and _____ grandchildren.
2. Pernilla is _____ and Susanna is _____.
3. Pernilla's son Leo is _____ and her other son, Samuel, is _____.
4. Susanna's oldest daughter is called _____ and she is _____ years old.
5. Susanna's other daughter is called Ellen and she's _____ years old.
6. Anne-Maj and Arne have known each other for _____ years and been married for _____.

A Extension exercise

Fill in the blanks in these new sentences with words you heard during Anne-Maj's interview. The words are listed in the box to help you.

> about   alive   also   close   flat   from
> married   middle   mum   only   own   quite
> remember   say   relationship   spell   study   top

1. I originally come _____ Boston, but I've spent most of my life in Chicago.
2. How do you _____ 'good morning' in Japanese?
3. How do you _____ ceiling? Is it c-i-e or c-e-i?
4. The attic is at the _____ of a house. It's the space under the roof.
5. I'm _____ hungry. Can we eat soon?
6. I can't wait to hear all _____ your holiday.
7. My brother Adam is _____ a teacher.
8. I can't _____ when Bruno's birthday is. Can you?
9. My parents got _____ in 1990 and I was born in 1992.
10. When I got my first job I rented a little one-bedroom _____ in the centre of Birmingham.
11. I quite like living on my _____ because you can do whatever you want.
12. He says he can't come out because he's in the _____ of his exams and he's got to _____.
13. I have a much better _____ with my brother now than when we were kids.
14. Our house is quite _____ to the station so we can pick you up if you like.
15. I've got four brothers so I'm the _____ girl.
16. My dad works in a law firm and my _____ is the manager of a sports centre.
17. Only one of my grandparents is still _____ — my mother's father who's 80 and lives in Baltimore.

B Family members

Fill in the gaps with words from the box. The words are listed in the box to help you.

> aunt   cousin   grandfather   grandmother   grandson
> nephew   niece   sister-in-law   uncle

1. My mother's father is my _____.
2. My father's sister is my _____.
3. My mother's brother is my _____.
4. My aunt's daughter is my _____.
5. My father's mother is my _____.
6. My sister's daughter is my _____.
7. My brother's wife is my _____.
8. My brother's son is my _____.
9. My daughter's son is my _____.

Part 1: Talking about her town in Sweden (47")

I: Um, Anne-Maj, you come from Sweden.
A–M: Yes.
I: Which um, part of Sweden do you come from?
A–M: From er, er, west . . .
I: West Sweden?
A–M: West Sweden.
I: How do you say that in Swedish?
A–M: Västra.
I: Västra Sverige.
A–M: Västra Sverige.
I: OK. And what's the name of the town you come from?
A–M: Trollhättan.
I: Oh, can you spell that for me, please?
A–M: T-R-O-L-L-H- Ä-T-T-A-N.
I: OK. So it's T-R-O-double L, H . . .
A–M: Yeah.
I: H . . . And then you said 'a', but do you mean a with two dots?
A–M: Yeah, yes.
I: So 'a' with two dots on top, double T-A-N.
A–M: Yes, that's right.

Part 2: Talking about her and her husband's family (5'43")

I: So I think you've got quite a big family.
A–M: Yes, I have.
I: Can you tell me about them?
A–M: I have three er, children.
I: Right.
A–M: Um, three girls: Annette, Marie, Camilla. Annette is er, 43 . . .
I: Mmm, hmm.
A–M: Um, Marie is 42 in September and Camilla is 39.
I: Right.
A–M: And I also have er, eight grandchildren.
I: Right.
A–M: Six boys and two girls.
I: Oh, that's nice. How old's the oldest?
A–M: Er, he's um, er, 22 in December.
I: OK.
A–M: And the youngest is 11.
I: Right. Can you remember their names?
A–M: Yeah.
I: So do it from youngest to oldest.
A–M: Youngest . . . Erika.

I: Mmm, hmm. How do you spell that — Erika?
A–M: E-R-E- [sic – I] K-A.
I: Erika. OK.
A–M: And er, Hannah, Daniel.
I: OK.
A–M: Magnus, Marcus, Patrik . . .
I: Yeah.
A–M: Mathias and Martin.
I: OK. The oldest boy — what's his name?
A–M: Martin.
I: Martin. Right. Has he got a girlfriend?
A–M: Yeah.
I: He has. Are they going to get married, do you think?
A–M: No, no. Not at the moment, anyway.
I: OK.
A–M: And er, er, a month ago he get [sic – got] his own (1) flat.
I: Mmm. That's very good . . .
A–M: Yeah.
I: . . . for someone so young. Is he buying it, or . . .
A–M: No.
I: Renting.
A–M: (2) He's renting.
I: But he's living on his own.
A–M: Yes . . .
I: OK.
A–M: . . . for the moment.
I: Right. Um, do you have brothers and sisters?
A–M: Yeah. I have er, two sisters and three bro . . . brothers.
I: Oh, so you come from a big family.
A–M: Yeah.
I: Where do you come in, in the family?
A–M: In the middle.
I: OK. So how old is your oldest brother or sister?
A–M: Er, my oldest brother is er, sixty . . . 67.
I: OK. And your youngest brother or sister?
A–M: Er, er, it's my brother. Er, my youngest brother is er, 53.
I: (3) Do you have a good relationship with your brothers and sisters?
A–M: Er, not, not very, very much relationships (*laughs*). [sic – we don't have a lot to do with each other]
I: Not very close.
A–M: No, not very close. Er . . .
I: Do, do you see any of them?
A–M: Yeah, I do, but it depends on . . . um . . . We don't er, live close to each other.
I: I see.

A-M: So um . . .

I: So none of them are in Trollhättan?

A-M: No, I'm the only one.

I: OK. Where, where did you come from to Trollhättan? Where were you born?

A-M: Er, 15 er, Swedish miles from Trollhättan.

I: OK.

A-M: . . . so um . . .

I: So a hundred and fifty kilometres.

A-M: Yes, it is.

I: OK.

A-M: In a town er, called er, Tidaholm.

I: How do you spell that?

A-M: T-I-D-A-H-O-L-M.

I: Right. So is that towards the east . . . the east of Sweden?

A-M: Yeah. It's more . . . more the er, middle, you can say, yeah.

I: Right. OK. So brothers and sisters. Are your mum and dad still alive?

A-M: No, (4) unfortunately.

I: And er, children, three girls and the eight grandchildren.

A-M: Yeah.

I: OK. Any other family?

A-M: The other family?

I: Do you have any other family?

A-M: Yeah – my husband's er, children.

I: OK.

A-M: Er, my husband Arne has two girls.

I: So between you you have five girls.

A-M: Yeah.

I: OK.

A-M: And um, er, his girls has [sic –his girls have] er, four children: two girls and two boys.

I: Right.

A-M: And they are um, quite little. The youngest one is um, three years and the oldest is er, 13.

I: Right. So he has two girls.

A-M: Yeah.

I: Do they each have a girl and a boy, or . . .?

A-M: Mmm?

I: Does, does, does one daughter have two boys and one daughter have two girls?

A-M: Yes, yes, yeah.

I: Oh, it's worked out like that. (*laughs*) Are they, Arne's children, younger or older than your children?

A-M: They are younger.

I: Younger.

A-M: Pernilla is um, 35.

I: Mhm, hmm.

A-M: And um, Susanna is er, 32.

I: OK. And how old are their children? How old are Pernilla's children?

A-M: Er, Pernilla's children are um . . . The youngest boy Leo is er, three and um, Samuel is er, six.

I: OK.

A-M: Yeah.

I: And the girls?

A-M: And there is um, Julia. She's 13.

I: Right.

A-M: And Ellen. She's 10.

I: OK. You said Julia. Er, how do you spell that?

A-M: J-U-L-E . . . I!-A

I: OK. So we'd say 'Julia', but you say 'Julia'.

A-M: Yeah.

I: How long have you been with Arne?

A-M: For er, 25 years.

I: OK.

A-M: We've been married for 22.

I: OK. That's quite a long time.

A-M: Yep.

---

5. Words and Phrases

1 **(a) flat** (BrE) (AmE **an apartment**) a set of rooms for living in, usually on one floor and part of a larger building

2 **He's renting.** – He pays a fixed amount of money for the use of the flat to the person or company which owns it. (i.e. He has not bought the flat.)

3 **Do you have a good relationship with your brothers and sisters?** – Do you get on well with your brothers and sisters?

4 **unfortunately** – (in this context) sadly

UNIT **5** Danny

1. Pre-Listening Comprehension

Danny is a student at Nottingham University. He spent a year in Dover on a placement as part of his studies. Danny comes from a small market town near Cambridge.

Normalisation

This exercise is designed to help you get used to Danny's voice. Listen to the first part of the interview and see how much you can understand.

Corrections

Correct the mistake in the following sentences.

1. Danny has got two brothers.

   _____

2. He has two younger sisters.

   _____

3. His sisters live with Danny's father.

   _____

4. His younger sister is 23.

   _____

5. His other sister is 20.

   _____

6. Danny is 29.

   _____

7. Nathalie works with old people.

   _____

8. Danny's dad has a sister.

   _____

9. Danny's uncle is a few years younger than his dad.

   _____

10. Danny's mother has three half-sisters.

   _____

11. Danny has two grandparents.

   _____

12. His mother's father is still alive.

   _____

13. A lot of Danny's cousins live in Australia.

   _____

14. Danny was planning to go to America this winter.

   _____

A Extension exercise

Fill in the blanks in these new sentences with words you heard during Danny's interview. The words are listed in the box to help you.

> cousins   few   get   moment   older   planning
> remember   side   strange   than   with

1. I've got three _____ in New Zealand. They're my mother's oldest brother's children.

2. My sister is three years _____ than me, so she's always telling me what to do.

3. I'm living _____ my parents at the _____, but I'm hoping to get my own place soon.

4. Do you _____ on well with your parents?

5. Is your brother older or younger _____ you?

6. I want to work for a _____ years before I go to university.

7. Can you _____ what time the library shuts on Saturdays?

8. Most of my family on my father's _____ live in Wales.

9. Don't you think Zack is a _____ name for a boy?

10. We're _____ on going to Australia next year so we need to save up.

B Prepositions and adverbs

Put the correct prepositions or adverbs in these sentences which are based on the interview. Some of them are used twice.

> about   at   in   of   on   to   up   with

1. Come and tell me all _____ your holiday. Did you have a good time?

2. I went _____ London last weekend _____ an old school-friend.

3. Would you like a bit _____ dessert? It's too much for me to eat.

4. Sorry, we're right _____ the middle of dinner. Can I call you back?

5. I get _____ better with my mother than my father.

6. My father grew _____ in Connecticut, but he moved _____ Boston when he was 20.

7. I've got a lot _____ homework to do, so I can't come out tonight.

8. We're planning _____ taking our parents to Athens this summer as a surprise.

9. I wanted to be doctor when I was young, but I ended _____ working in a supermarket.

10. I'm feeling a lot better _____ the moment. I think it's because I'm eating healthier and doing more exercise.

I: OK, can you um, tell me something about your family? Because I don't know how many brothers and sisters you've got, cousins, whatever. Can, can you talk about them?

D: I have two sisters.

I: Right.

D: One older, one younger.

I: Mmm, hmm.

D: Er, they both live with my mother at the moment, through a bit of bad luck, **(1) unfortunately. (2) Hence,** um . . . But my older sister's 23, coming up 24. And my younger sister's 19.

I: How old are you?

D: I am 21.

I: Oh.

D: (*laughs*)

I: So you're right in the middle.

D: **(3) I'm right in the middle, smack-bang.** And um, Nathalie, my oldest . . . the older sister is . . . She works with children, so she cares for children and does a lot of work for them. And my younger sister, Michelle, er, works at **(4) Tesco's** . . .

I: Mmm.

D: . . . **Superstores.**

I: Right. OK. **(5) Do you get on with them both?**

D: I get on very well with them now. I never used to.

I: Right.

D: I think probably just **(6) sibling conflict** (*laughs*). When you're younger and growing up.

I: Mmm. What, what about your mum and dad? Have they got lots of brothers and sisters?

D: Um, my dad has a brother. Both his parents are dead now.

I: Right.

D: But he's, he's got a brother, um, but that's the only **(7) close relative** I would say that he has now, um . . .

I: Mmm. Is he older or younger than your dad?

D: Than my mum?

I: Than your dad.

D: Oh, my . . . my uncle?

I: Yeah.

D: He's older . . .

I: Right.

D: . . . um, by a few years, only a few years older.

I: Mmm.

D: My mother um, she has, let me try and think . . . She has one sister . . . No, no, she has two half-sisters, that's the one. She has two half-sisters from a different father.

I: Right. So her father re-married?

D: Different mother. No. (*laughs*) Her mother re-married.

I: Re-married. OK. All right. Have you got grandparents?

D: One still alive.

I: OK.

D: (*laughs*) **(8) All of the others passed away.**

I: Oh, dear. Is, is the one who's still alive, is that your mother's father, or?

D: My mother's mother.

I: Mother's mother.

D: Yeah.

I: Mmm, hmm. Do you have um, any cousins?

D: Plenty.

I: Really?

D: I can't remember them.

I: How many have you got, then?

D: A lot, I think. Most of them on my mother's side. But they live in America. A lot of them live in America, I think. But I do have a lot of cousins. Can't remember their names, either. You know how Americans are — they like to give their children strange names.

I: Yes. Have you ever been over to America to see them?

D: Not yet. I was planning on going this summer, but **(9) it fell through. (10) Visa trouble.**

I: Mmm. Oh, **(11) that's a shame. (12) So you ended up working here.**

D: (*laughs*) Yeah!

5. Words and Phrases

1   **unfortunately** – unluckily, as in 'Unfortunately I missed my train.'
2   **Hence** – (normally used in formal or written English) That is the reason . . .
3   **I'm right in the middle, smack–bang.** – I'm exactly in the middle.
4   **Tesco's Superstores** – a big supermarket chain
5   **Do you get on with them both?** – Do you have a good relationship with them both?
6   **sibling conflict** – when brothers and sisters fight because they both want attention (normally called 'sibling rivalry')
7   **close relative** – someone who is a direct relation: mother, father, uncle, etc. (for example not your father's cousin's son-in-law's brother)
8   **All of the others passed away.** – All the others died. All the others are dead.
9   **it fell through** – it didn't happen
10 **Visa trouble.** – Danny had problems getting a visa which he needed to travel to the USA.
11 **that's a shame** – that's a pity (meaning that was unlucky)
12 **So you ended up working here.** – So finally, after all that, you came to work here.

A Typical Day

UNIT 6 Dorothy

This is an interview with Dorothy, a retired headmistress, talking about a typical day. Dorothy originally comes from Heckmondwike in Yorkshire in the North of England, but she moved to London when she married her husband Dennis in the 1950s. She has a neutral accent and speaks slowly and clearly.

A Normalisation – sentence stress

This exercise is designed to help you get used to Dorothy's voice. Speakers stress the words they feel are important to convey their meaning. Underline the words you expect Dorothy to stress in the following extracts, then listen to check your answers.

1. if you're interested in what my husband has . . .
2. and two slices of toast with marmalade on them
3. And if it's raining, I might do some housework.
4. if it's a shopping day we go out and do our shopping together
5. we always take a list
6. we have our evening meal quite early

B Normalisation – anticipating the next word

Listen to tracks 94–98. There is a word missing from the end of each excerpt. Try to guess the missing word and write it down. Then listen to track 99 to check your answers. How well did you guess?

1. _____
2. _____
3. _____
4. _____
5. _____

A Part 1 – Ticking boxes

Tick (✓) the correct box.

1. Dorothy gets up at about _____ o'clock.

☐ six   ☐ eight   ☐ nine

2. She generally has a _____.

☐ bath   ☐ shower

3. At home she usually wears _____.

☐ a skirt   ☐ trousers

4. For breakfast she has _____.

☐ an apple   ☐ an orange   ☐ a banana

5. She has _____ slice(s) of toast.

☐ one   ☐ two   ☐ three

6. She also has a _____.

☐ cup of tea   ☐ cup of coffee

B Part 2 – Ticking boxes

Tick (✓) the correct box.

1. After breakfast Dorothy reads _____.

☐ a book   ☐ a magazine   ☐ the newspaper

2. She reads for _____ minutes.

☐ 30   ☐ 20   ☐ 10

3. At 11 o'clock, Dorothy and her husband have a _____.

☐ glass of orange juice   ☐ cup of tea   ☐ cup of coffee

4. Then they do a crossword for no more than _____ minutes.

☐ 5   ☐ 10   ☐ 15

5. For lunch they often just have _____.

☐ a hamburger   ☐ a sandwich   ☐ a banana

C Part 3 – Ticking boxes

Tick (✓) the correct box.

1. The supermarket they go to is about _____ miles away.

   ☐ two ☐ three ☐ five

2. In the afternoon Dorothy often _____.

   ☐ listens to music ☐ uses the computer ☐ reads a book

3. Dorothy and her husband have dinner at about _____ o'clock.

   ☐ five ☐ half-past six ☐ seven

4. They often have _____ with dinner.

   ☐ a glass of wine ☐ a glass of water ☐ a cup of tea.

5. They go to bed at about _____.

   ☐ 10 to 10.30pm ☐ 11 to 11.30pm ☐ 11.30 to midnight

A The present simple

Because Dorothy is talking about her daily routine, she frequently uses the present simple. Look at these excerpts:

I get up at about eight o'clock.
I usually have a shower.
I always clean and cream my face.

We often use these adverbs of frequency with the present simple:
usually, often, sometimes, normally, generally, never.

B *depending on*

Dorothy says:

*Then I decide what I'm going to wear, **depending on** the weather.*
This means that if the weather's cold she wears warm clothes and if it's hot she wears summer clothes. Here are some more examples of ***depending on***:

'We will either go by train or by plane, depending on the price.'
'I should be home at six o'clock, depending on the traffic.'

C *might* for possibility

Dorothy says that if she's going out *I **might** wear a skirt.* This means there is a possibility she will wear a skirt, but it's not definite.

She also says:

*In the evening we **might** sit and watch television, if there's anything interesting to watch.*

Again, Dorothy is talking about possibility. It is possible that there will be something interesting on television, but it's not definite.

Here are some more examples:

'I might go to India next year, if I have enough money.'
'Peter might be at the party.'
'I think it might snow tomorrow.'

D **Reduced syllables in spoken English**

Look at the following words and mark how many syllables they contain when spoken in isolation:

interested (___) *probably* (___) *perhaps* (___) *interesting* (___)

Now listen to these extracts from the interview and mark how many syllables the words listed above contain in a stream of speech.

1. Um, if you're *interested* (___) in what my husband has . . .

2. And I will use . . . read that usually for oh, *probably* (___) half an hour.

3. *Perhaps* (___) I should explain that we are retired, so that our time is our own . . .

4. And then in the evening um, we might sit and watch television, if there's anything *interesting* (___) to watch.

A Hearing the sounds of English 1

Listen and repeat each minimal pair after the speaker.

skirt/shirt	list/wrist
cup/cub	room/loom
bowl/pole	card/cart
clean/cream	bed/bet
wheel/veal	sleep/slip

B Discriminating between minimal pairs of sounds 1

Listen and underline the words you hear.

1. I like your new **skirt/shirt**.
2. What a beautiful **cub/cup**!
3. Here's your **pole/bowl**.
4. I always **clean/cream** my face before I go to bed.
5. I can't see the **wheel/veal**.
6. Have you seen my **list/wrist**?
7. What a big **loom/room**!
8. Where's the **cart/card**?
9. I don't know where to place my **bet/bed**.
10. The name of the film is The Big **Slip/Sleep**.

C Intonation – falling intonation for statements

When we make a statement in English our voice falls at the end of the statement. This also indicates that the speaker has finished talking. Listen to Dorothy making the following statements and mark where her voice begins to fall, as in the first example:

1. my breakfast never varies

2. the porridge is, is good for him

3. we go out and do our shopping together

4. I sit and read the paper.

5. We take the Guardian.

Now make some statements about yourself using this intonation pattern, such as:

I live in Bury.　　　I am 20 years old.　　　I work in a shop.

D Recognising individual words in a stream of speech 1 – dictation

  to

Work with a partner. Listen to the excerpts from Dorothy's interview and write them down. Then check your answers with another pair.

1. _____

2. _____

3. _____

4. _____

5. _____

6. _____

7. _____

E Contractions

Contractions are common in informal spoken and written English, such as two friends chatting, emails between friends, and so on, but not in more formal English such as lectures, speeches and letters to companies.

The following contractions appear in the interview:

do not – *don't*	it is – *it's*
does not – *doesn't*	that is – *that's*
he has/he is – *he's*	there is – *there's*
I am – *I'm*	we are – *we're*
I have – *I've*	you are – *you're*
is not – *isn't*	

Look at the following excerpts from the interview and put in the appropriate contractions. Then listen and check your answers.

1. I always um, clean and cream my face, because _____ supposed to be a good thing for your skin, so I _____ forget to do that.

2. Then I decide what _____ going to wear . . .

3. Um, if _____ interested in what my husband has . . .

4. Um, when _____ read the paper then _____ the point when I decide what _____ going to do for the day.

5. And if _____ raining, I might do some housework.

6. If it _____ raining, I _____ want to waste time indoors . . .

7. the house _____ get very dirty because _____ only my husband and I um, to make a mess in it

8. it takes about 10 minutes because _____ a very easy crossword

9. We _____ usually have lunch.

10. Um, if _____ a shopping day we go out and do our shopping together.

11. We always take a list so that _____ not wasting time . . .

12. we might sit and watch television, if _____ anything interesting to watch

F   **Recognising individual words in a stream of speech 2 – elision**

When speaking quickly in English, people often miss out individual sounds at the ends of words – a process known as elision. For example, a speaker will say *las' night* instead of *last night*, *jus' got here* instead of *just got here*, or *trie' to* instead of *tried to*.

Listen and fill in the missing words in these extracts, all of which have been affected by elision.

1. my _____ never varies

2. Summer _____ winter?

3. _____ paper do you get?

4. they get _____ more frequently than the rest of the house

5. a _____ drink

6. We have it at about half-_____ six.

7. I tend to alternate between a cooked meal one day and a salad meal the _____ day.

G Hearing the sounds of English 2

As with Exercise A, listen and repeat each minimal pair after the speaker.

right/light	has/as
always/hallways	sit/seat
tend/tent	time/tame

H Discriminating between minimal pairs of sounds 2

Tick (✓) the boxes which correspond to the words you hear.

1	1	2	3	4	5
right					
light					
2	1	2	3	4	5
always					
hallways					
3	1	2	3	4	5
tend					
tent					
4	1	2	3	4	5
has					
as					
5	1	2	3	4	5
sit					
seat					
6	1	2	3	4	5
time					
tame					

I **Recognising individual words in a stream of speech 3 – weak forms**

This gap-fill consists of excerpts from the interview and contains words which you should know, but may have problems recognising in a stream of speech.

Before you listen try to fill in the missing words. Then listen and check your answers.

1. So, Dorothy, _____ you tell me about a typical day?

2. that's supposed to be a good thing _____ your skin, so I don't forget _____ do that

3. we have breakfast around a quarter _____ nine

4. the porridge is, is good _____ _____

5. _____ paper do you get?

6. that's the point when I decide what I'm _____ to do _____ the day

7. I might do _____ housework.

8. so I go out _____ do something in the garden

9. they get cleaned more frequently _____ the rest _____ the house

10. And I make coffee _____ both _____ us.

11. We always take a list so _____ we're not wasting time . . .

12. We _____ often _____ a glass _____ wine er, with our, our evening meal.

13. we might sit _____ watch television . . .

14. And er, usually that's enough _____ send us off _____ sleep.

J Recognising individual words in a stream of speech 4 – linking

When a word ends in a consonant in spoken English and the next word begins with a vowel, the end of the first word will often link with the start of the second word.

Example:

> I have **an_orange**, two **slices_of** toast . . .

Mark where you think linking will take place in the following excerpts from the interview, then listen and check your answers.

1. a cup of coffee
2. I sit and read the paper.
3. there's only my husband and I um, to make a mess in it
4. it takes about 10 minutes because it's a very easy crossword
5. a drink of something
6. We go to the supermarket which is about three miles away . . .
7. We have it at about half-past six.
8. usually that's enough to send us off to sleep

A Gap–fill

This is a revision exercise. You will probably be able to complete it correctly, even without hearing the extract again. The missing words are listed in the box to help you.

Take a few minutes to try to predict the missing words before you listen.

> book cup drink early easy evening glass half home
> husband list make miles my often sit supermarket
> takes together usually vegetables watch

Dorothy:

So at about 11 o'clock I will usually say to my **(1)** _____, 'Would you like a **(2)** _____ of coffee?' And I **(3)** _____ coffee for both of us. And then we **(4)** _____ down together and do the Quick Crossword in The Guardian newspaper which, on a bad day, it **(5)** _____ about 10 minutes because it's a very **(6)** _____ crossword.

Um, we don't **(7)** _____ have lunch. Um, we might have a banana at lunchtime and a **(8)** _____ of something, a soft drink or, or tea or coffee.

Um, if it's a shopping day we go out and do our shopping **(9)** _____. We go to the **(10)** _____ which is about three **(11)** _____ away, and um, we wheel the trolley round together. We always take a **(12)** _____ so that we're not wasting time and er, find when we get **(13)** _____ that we've forgotten something.

And er, and then um, what do we do then? Um, well **(14)** _____ husband will **(15)** _____ disappear upstairs to do things on the computer. And I will often settle myself down in the sitting room with a **(16)** _____.

Um, we have our **(17)** _____ meal quite **(18)** _____. We have it at about **(19)** _____-past six. And, um, I tend to alternate between a cooked meal one day and a salad meal the next day. So we eat quite a lot of salad and quite a lot of **(20)** _____. Um, and we will often have a **(21)** _____ of wine er, with our, our evening meal.

And then in the evening, um, we might sit and **(22)** _____ television, if there's anything interesting to watch.

B Extension exercise   Fill in the blanks with words you heard during Dorothy's interview. The missing words are listed in the box to help you.

bowl	clean	dirty	forget	get	housework	list
mess	retired	salad	shower	slices	takes	tidy

1. We _____ up at about 10 o'clock on Sundays.

2. My husband always has a bath in the morning, but I prefer a _____.

3. He always forgets to _____ the bath afterwards.

4. Don't _____ to get some milk!

5. My father _____ when he was 65, but before that he worked in a factory.

6. How many _____ of toast do you want?

7. I have a _____ of cornflakes for breakfast every morning.

8. The only _____ I like is ironing. I can't stand cleaning or polishing.

9. My daughter keeps her room very _____ — everything is always in its place.

10. Your shoes are very _____ — can you take them off, please?

11. I'm sorry I made a _____ in the kitchen — I'll clean it up in a minute.

12. It _____ about 10 minutes to walk to the shops from here.

13. "Hi, Clare. I'm in the supermarket but I've forgotten the shopping _____. What do we need?"

14. Would you like a cooked meal, or shall we just have some _____ as it's so hot?

C Prepositions and adverbs

Put the correct preposition or adverb in these sentences which are based on the interview. Some of them are used more than once.

> for   in   of   on   up   with

1. What time do you normally get _____ on a Sunday?
2. I'm just going to put _____ a warmer jacket.
3. We're hoping to have a barbecue, but it depends _____ the weather.
4. Could I have another slice _____ toast, please?
5. You should meet my sister. She's really interested _____ politics, too.
6. Have some more carrots. They're good _____ you.
7. What would you like to drink _____ dinner?
8. I was really lazy yesterday. I stayed _____ bed all morning.
9. I think James is in his room playing games _____ his computer.

D Transformations

Change the word in each bracket which Dorothy used in her interview to form a word which fits the gap.

1. We're not expecting rain — just a few (shower) _____.
2. My boyfriend's mother is very house-proud. She's always (clean) _____ the kitchen when I go round.
3. Oh no! I've (forget) _____ to buy Sam a birthday present.
4. Can you put another slice of bread in the (toast) _____ for me?
5. This book's really (interested) _____. You must read it after me.
6. There are more (weeding) _____ than flowers in my garden!
7. If you're a (frequently) _____ flyer then you can get cheaper plane tickets.
8. Hurry up! There's no time to (wasting) _____!
9. I love (cooked) _____, but I never seem to get to do any these days.
10. His new girlfriend's a (vegetables) _____ which is a bit difficult when we have them over for dinner.
11. Sorry, can I call you back? I'm (watch) _____ a really interesting programme on television.

E Matching words with definitions

Match the definitions with the words in the box which are taken from the interview.

> dirty   face   housework   marmalade   a mile   skin
> a soft drink   a supermarket   toast   weeds

1. Something which covers your whole body, from head to foot: _____
2. The front of your head: _____
3. Bread made warm, brown and crisp by being near a high heat: _____
4. A kind of jam made from oranges: _____
5. Cooking, cleaning, ironing, etc.: _____
6. The unwanted plants which grow in a garden: _____
7. The opposite of clean: _____
8. A non-alcoholic drink: _____
9. A shop which sells food items and items for the home where the customer takes things from the shelves and pays at a till: _____
10. A unit of distance equal to 1.6 kilometres: _____

I: So, Dorothy, can you tell me about a typical day?

D: Yes, OK. Um, I get up about eight o'clock and er, I usually have a shower. And then um, **(1) I always um, clean and cream my face**, because that's supposed to be a good thing for your **(2) skin**, so I don't forget to do that. Um, then I decide what I'm going to wear, depending on the weather. Most of the time, now that I'm **(3) retired**, I tend to wear trousers and **(4) a top**. If I'm going out I might put on a skirt. Um, we have breakfast around a quarter to nine, nine o'clock. And, um, **(5) my breakfast never varies**. I have an orange, two slices of toast with **(6) tuna pâté** on them and a cup of coffee. Um, if you're interested in what my husband has, he has **(7) a bowl of porridge**, and two slices of toast with **(8) marmalade** on them and a cup of tea.

I: Always?

D: Always.

I: Summer and winter?

D: Yes, because um, the er, the porridge is, is good for him. That's why he has the porridge. Um, then after breakfast um, I sit and read the paper.

I: What paper do you get?

D: We take **(9) The Guardian**. And I will use . . . read that usually for oh, probably half an hour. Perhaps I should explain that we are retired, so that our time is our own . . .

I: Right.

D: . . . and **(10) we can do what we like** with it. Um, when I've read the paper then that's the point when I decide what I'm going to do for the day. And if it's raining, I might do some **(11) housework**. If it isn't raining, **(12) I don't want to waste time indoors**, so I go out and do something in the garden — **(13) a bit of weeding** or er, **(14) pruning** or generally **(15) keeping the garden (16) tidy**. Um, I have decided that as a retired person there is no way that I should have to um, clean the whole house **(17) in one go**, so one day I might clean downstairs and another day I might clean upstairs. And the only um, exception to that rule is the bathrooms, and they get cleaned more frequently than the rest of the house. **(18) In any case**, the **house doesn't get very (19) dirty** because there's only my husband and I um, **(20) to make a mess** in it. So at about 11 o'clock I will usually say to my husband, 'Would you like a cup of coffee?' And I make coffee for both of us. And then we sit down together and do the Quick **(21) Crossword** in The Guardian newspaper which, on a bad day, it takes about 10 minutes because it's a very easy crossword. Um, we don't usually have lunch. Um, we might have a banana at lunchtime and a drink of something, **(22) a soft drink** or, or tea or coffee. Um, if it's a shopping day we go out and do our shopping together. We go to the supermarket which is about three miles away, and um, **(23) we wheel the (24) trolley round together**. We always take **(25) a list** so that we're not wasting time and er, find when we get home that we've forgotten something. And er, and then um, what do we do then? Um, well **(26) my husband will often disappear upstairs** to do things on the computer. And **(27) I will often settle myself down in the sitting room with a book**. Um, we have our evening meal quite early. We have it at about half-past six. And, um, **(28) I tend to alternate between a cooked meal one day and a salad meal the next day**. So we eat quite a lot of salad and quite a lot of vegetables. Um, and we will often have a glass of wine er, with our, our evening meal. And then in the evening, um, we might sit and watch television, if there's anything interesting to watch. If there isn't, we might play a game of **(29) cribbage** or another card game. Um, we go to bed well, not too early. Around 11, 11.30. But always, before we settle down to go to sleep, **(30) we tackle the big Guardian crossword**.

I: Oh, right.

D: We, we do that in bed rather than doing it, you know, during the day. And er, usually that's enough to send us off to sleep. And if we haven't finished it, we finish it the following morning.

I: I see, OK, thank you very much.

1. **I always clean and cream my face** – Instead of washing her face with soap and water Dorothy uses a cleansing lotion, which is better for her skin. She then puts skin cream on her face.
2. **skin** – the surface of your body
3. **retired** – A retired person is someone who has finished their working life.
4. **a top** – for example a jumper, a blouse, a T-shirt, a vest
5. **my breakfast never varies** – my breakfast never changes; I always have the same breakfast
6. **tuna pâté** – a smooth, soft paste made from tuna fish
7. **a bowl of porridge** – Porridge is a hot, soft breakfast food made by boiling crushed oats with milk and/or water.
8. **marmalade** – a type of jam made from citrus fruit (usually oranges, but it can be grapefruit, limes, lemons, etc.) usually eaten at breakfast
9. **The Guardian** – a left-wing, quality newspaper
10. **we can do what we like** – we can do what we want
11. **housework** – work that you do to look after the home, e.g. cleaning, washing clothes, ironing, washing up, dusting, making the beds, etc.
12. **I don't want to waste time indoors** – I don't want to make a bad use of my time by staying indoors.
13. **a bit of weeding** – pulling up unwanted wild plants from the garden
14. **pruning** – cutting back some of the branches of bushes and trees to make them grow better
15. **keeping the garden tidy** – keeping the garden under control
16. **tidy** – neatly arranged with everything in the right place
17. **in one go** – all at once, all at the same time
18. **In any case, the house doesn't get very dirty** – anyway, the house doesn't become very dirty
19. **dirty** – unclean, marked with dirt
20. **to make a mess** – to make a place very untidy or dirty
21. **(a) crossword** – a word game in which you write the answers to puzzles in a pattern of numbered boxes
22. **a soft drink** – a cold, non-alcoholic drink such as juice or Sprite
23. **we wheel the trolley round together** – we push the trolley around together
24. **(a) trolley** – a large metal shopping basket on wheels
25. **a list** – (normally **a shopping list**) – all the things you need to buy written one below the other
26. **my husband will often disappear upstairs** – my husband will often go upstairs and I don't see him for a long time
27. **I will often settle myself down in the sitting room with a book** – I will often go into the sitting room, sit down comfortably and read.
28. **I tend to alternate between a cooked meal one day and a salad meal the next day** – I usually prepare a cooked meal one day and make a salad the next.
29. **cribbage** – a card game played with a wooden board and small pieces of wood to show how many points you have won
30. **we tackle the big Guardian crossword** – we try to do the big Guardian crossword

UNIT 7 Peter

This is an interview with Peter, an engineer who has lived in north–east London all his life. Peter has a strong London accent.

A Normalisation – two typical features of a London accent

Peter lives in Walthamstow in East London and he speaks with a strong London accent. Two typical features of a Cockney accent are dropping the initial *h-* and also saying *an'* instead of *and*. (Remember these features can also occur in other regional accents.)

Put a line through the letters *h* and *d* where Peter doesn't pronounce the initial *h-* of some words and where he doesn't pronounce the *-d* of *and*.

1. Leave home, drive to Stevenage in Hertfordshire . . .
2. read my post and then start whatever's at hand for the day
3. So something between 12 and two, normally.
4. And then back in the car . . .
5. I normally have a cup of tea . . .
6. Then I go and have a shower or a bath . . .
7. take up some strange habits and hobbies down there
8. between half-eleven and 12 o'clock

B Normalisation – anticipating the next word

 to

Listen to tracks 124–128. There is a word missing from the end of each excerpt. Try to guess the missing word and write it down. Then listen to track 129 to check your answers. How well did you guess?

1. _____
2. _____
3. _____
4. _____
5. _____

A Part 1 – Ticking boxes   Tick (✓) the correct box.

(130)

1. Peter gets up at _____.

    ☐ 6.45am   ☐ 7.45am   ☐ 8.45am

2. He has a _____.

    ☐ shower   ☐ bath   ☐ wash

3. He leaves home at _____.

    ☐ 7.45am   ☐ 8am   ☐ 8.15am

4. He _____ to work.

    ☐ walks   ☐ cycles   ☐ drives

5. He arrives at work at about _____.

    ☐ 8.30am   ☐ 8.45am   ☐ 9am

6. As soon as he gets to work he usually switches on _____.

    ☐ the lights   ☐ the kettle   ☐ his computer

7. He has _____ for lunch.

    ☐ 30 minutes   ☐ 45 minutes   ☐ an hour

8. He usually has lunch between _____.

    ☐ 12 and 1pm   ☐ 12 and 2pm   ☐ 1 and 2 pm

B Part 2 – Ticking boxes

Tick (✓) the correct box.

1. Peter usually leaves work between _____.

   ☐ 4.30 and 5pm   ☐ 5 and 5.30pm   ☐ 5:30 and 6pm

2. When he gets home he normally has a _____.

   ☐ cup of tea   ☐ can of beer   ☐ cup of coffee

3. He talks to his _____.

   ☐ children   ☐ wife   ☐ girlfriend

4. He has dinner between _____.

   ☐ 6 and 6.30pm   ☐ 6.30 and 7pm   ☐ 7 and 7.30pm

5. After dinner he _____.

   ☐ reads a book   ☐ watches television   ☐ listens to music

6. He goes to bed between _____.

   ☐ 10 and 10.30pm   ☐ 11 and 11.30pm   ☐ 11.30 and midnight

3. Interesting Language Points

A The present simple for talking about routines

As in the interview with Dorothy, Peter mainly uses the present simple to talk about his routine, together with common adverbs of frequency.

I normally get up about quarter to seven.
normally I always have a cup of tea ...
I'm normally ready to leave home about seven forty-five
I'll normally eat round about seven o'clock ...

B *It depends on* (something)

We use *depends on* when the answer varies, or when the answer is dependent on something else.

Peter says:

I normally leave work between five and five-thirty. It depends on the workload of the day.

This means that if he has a lot of work to do then he leaves work late. If he doesn't have a lot of work to do, then he leaves work early. Here are some more examples of *It depends on*:

Q: 'What time do you usually get home?'
A: 'It depends on the traffic.'

Q: 'Shall we have a barbecue tomorrow?'
A: 'It depends on the weather.'

Later in the interview Peter says he goes to bed between half-eleven and 12 o'clock.

He then says:

It does depend, though.

Again the meaning is that the answer varies: sometimes he goes to bed later than 11.30 to 12, and sometimes he goes to bed earlier than 11.30 to 12.

A Recognising individual words in a stream of speech 1 – dictation

 to

Work with a partner. Listen to the excerpts from Peter's interview and write them down. Then check your answers with another pair.

1. _____

2. _____

3. _____

4. _____

5. _____

B Making the 'er' sound when pausing

When people are talking they often say 'er' while they are giving themselves time to think about what they are going to say next. This can be confusing because 'er' sounds like 'a'.

What sound(s) do people make in your language when they are pausing? Listen to the following excerpts and mark where Peter uses 'er', as in the example.

Example:

  1. I normally get up about er, quarter, quarter to seven.

Exercise:

  2. I'm normally ready to leave home about seven forty-five.

  3. I do have a lunch break but it's half an hour . . .

  4. I have a workshop . . .

C Hearing the sounds of English 1

Listen and repeat each minimal pair after the speaker.

wash/watch	back/pack
work/walk	bath/path
hungry/angry	

D Discriminating between minimal pairs of sounds 1

Listen and underline the words you hear.

1. You must **wash/watch** this.
2. This **work/walk** is very hard.
3. I am very **angry/hungry**.
4. This is the **back/pack**.
5. What a long **bath/path**!

E Sentence stress

 to

Speakers stress the words they feel are important to convey their meaning. Underline the words you expect Peter to stress in the following extracts, then listen and check your answers.

1. Leave home, drive to Stevenage in Hertfordshire.
2. locate myself at my desk, and switch on the computer, look at emails, read my post
3. It's not at a regular time.
4. from the time I get hungry to the time I'm not
5. And then back in the car, back down the motorway.
6. I normally have a cup of tea, a chat with the wife.
7. Watch telly for an hour or so. Then I go and have a shower or a bath and watch some more telly!
8. sometimes I do other things

F Recognising individual words in a stream of speech 2 – weak forms

This gap-fill consists of excerpts from the interview and contains words which you should know, but may have problems recognising in a stream of speech. Before you listen try to fill in the missing words. Then listen and check your answers.

1. quarter _____ seven
2. have a cup _____ tea and _____ to eat
3. and arrive _____ work approximately nine, nine o'clock
4. locate myself _____ _____ desk
5. look _____ emails, read _____ post
6. It's not _____ a regular time.

7. It can _____ anything between . . . from . . . well, _____ the time I get hungry _____ the time I'm not.

8. back _____ Walthamstow _____ about six-thirty

9. Watch telly _____ an hour or so.

10. I have er, a workshop _____ I disappear to _____ time _____ time.

G Contractions

Contractions are common in informal spoken and written English, such as two friends chatting, emails between friends, and so on, but not in more formal English such as lectures, speeches and letters to companies.

The following contractions appear in the interview:

I am – *I'm*   it is – *it's*   that is – *that's*

Look at the following excerpts from the interview and put in the appropriate contractions. Then listen and check your answers.

1. _____ normally ready to leave home about er, seven forty-five.

2. . . . and it varies. _____ not at a regular time.

3. from the time I get hungry to the time _____ not

4. until I feel _____ time to come back

5. _____ the average.

H Hearing the sounds of English 2

As with Exercise C, listen and repeat each minimal pair after the speaker.

leave/leaf
hand/and
choose/shoes
feel/file

I Discriminating between minimal pairs of sounds 2

Tick (✓) the boxes which correspond to the words you hear.

1	1	2	3	4	5
leave					
leaf					
2	1	2	3	4	5
hand					
and					
3	1	2	3	4	5
choose					
shoes					
4	1	2	3	4	5
feel					
file					

J The glottal stop

Another feature of natural spoken English is the glottal stop. The glottal stop occurs when the speaker constricts his or her throat and blocks the air stream completely. This results in the speaker not pronouncing fully the *–t* sound at the end of words such as *got* or *lot*, or the *–t–* sounds in words such as *bottle* or *kettle*.

This gap-fill exercise focuses on words which you probably know already, but whose pronunciation has changed because of Peter's use of the glottal stop.

1. a _____ breakfast

2. and then _____ _____ at hand for the day

3. Well, yes, I do have a lunch break, _____ it's er, half an hour and _____ varies . . .

4. It's _____ at a regular time.

5. from the time I _____ hungry to the time I'm _____

6. and then I'll normally _____ round about seven o'clock . . .

7. until I feel it's time to come _____ ready for bed

A Extension exercise

Fill in the blanks with words you heard during Peter's interview. The words are listed in the box to help you. Some of them are used twice.

> approximately   chat   choose
> don't   hungry   ready   switch

1. I'm really _____. Can I have a sandwich, please?
2. It's very dark in here. Can you _____ on the light?
3. Shall we have tea or coffee? You _____.
4. I usually phone my mother for a _____ every Thursday.
5. Are you _____ to leave? Omar's waiting in the car.
6. I have lunch at _____ one o'clock.
7. We _____ normally go out in the evenings.
8. I need you to help me _____ what to wear for my interview on Friday.
9. If you're _____ make yourself some toast.
10. Our plane leaves at 10, so we must be _____ to leave here at six o'clock.
11. Can you _____ on the television?
12. I _____ like dogs, but I love cats.

B Prepositions

Fill in the missing prepositions in these sentences based on Peter's interview.

1. Could I have another cup _____ coffee, please?
2. I don't know if I'm going to have lunch today. It depends _____ how busy we are.
3. We didn't get _____ until 10 o'clock this morning, so we'd slept _____ nearly 10 hours.
4. There wasn't much traffic so we arrived _____ the airport nearly three hours early.
5. I'm going _____ bed. I've got a busy day tomorrow.
6. Would you like a chat _____ your dad? He's just got in.

7. We're going shopping _____ the morning. Do you need anything?
8. Could you switch _____ the light? It's a bit dark.
9. Come and look _____ this photo of James. It's brilliant.

C Transformations

Change the word in each bracket which Peter used in his interview to form a word which fits the gap.

1. I'm doing some (wash) _____ later. Have you got any dirty clothes?
2. We've stopped (eat) _____ chocolate because we're trying to lose weight.
3. Petra's got her (drive) _____ test next week. I hope she passes this time.
4. I (switch) _____ on my computer yesterday and nothing happened, so I had to call an engineer out.
5. You've got a (choose) _____ of sandwiches – ham, cheese or beef.
6. I (leave) _____ work early today because of the snow.
7. The (soon) _____ you go to the dentist the better.
8. This book is really (interests) _____. You'll have to read it after me.
9. Police are investigating the (disappear) _____ of a 17-year-old girl from Devon.
10. How are you (feel) _____? Have you got over your cold?

I: Can you tell me about a typical day?

P: Yes. I, I normally get up about er, quarter, quarter to seven. Um, wash. Don't shower or bath in the morning. Um, I wash. I then . . . normally I always have a cup of tea and something to eat, some . . . **(1) a light breakfast.** I'm normally **(2) ready** to leave home about er, seven forty-five. Leave home, drive to Stevenage in Hertfordshire and arrive at work approximately nine, nine o'clock. Um, well, I'll normally make a cup of tea, **(3) locate myself at my desk,** and **(4) switch on** the computer, look at emails, read my post **(5) and then start whatever's at hand for the day.**

I: Do you get a lunch break?

P: Not off . . . well, yes, I do have a lunch break, but it's er, half an hour and **(6) it varies.** It's not at a regular time. It can be anything between . . . from . . . well, from the time I get hungry to the time I'm not.

I: OK.

P: So something between 12 and two, normally.

I: Um, do you have to take your lunch between those hours?

P: No, no, no.

I: You can choose.

P: I, **(7) I can choose. (8) I'm very flexible.**

I: What time do you leave work?

P: I normally leave work between five and five-thirty. **(9) It depends on the workload of the day.** But normally it'll be . . . I would leave by five-fifteen, five-twenty. And then back in the car, back down **(10) the motorway,** back to Walthamstow for about six-thirty.

I: And do you have dinner as soon as you get home?

P: Not immediately. I normally have a cup of tea, **(11) a chat with** the wife, and then I'll normally eat round about seven o'clock, seven-thirty.

I: And what do you do then? Watch telly?

P: Watch **(12) telly** for an hour or so. Then I go and have a shower or a bath and watch some more telly! Not every night, though. Er, sometimes I do other things.

I: Like what?

P: Well, I have other interests. I have er, **(13) a workshop** that **(14) I disappear to** from time to time, **(15) take up some strange habits and hobbies** down there um, until I feel it's time to come back, ready for bed.

I: What time do you go to bed?

P: Normally 12 o'clock, between half-eleven and 12 o'clock. It does depend, though. **(16) That's the average.**

1. **a light breakfast** – not a big breakfast, just a piece of toast or a small bowl of cornflakes, etc.
2. **ready** – prepared
3. **locate myself at my desk** – (old-fashioned and very formal; often when people are recorded they use a more formal register) sit at my desk
4. **(to) switch on** – to turn on
5. **and then start whatever's at hand for the day** – and then begin whatever I need to do during the day
6. **it varies** – it changes from day to day
7. **I can choose.** – I can decide.
8. **I'm very flexible.** – (in this interview) I can eat earlier or later if necessary. It's not a problem.
9. **It depends on the workload of the day.** – (in this interview) If I have a lot of work to do, I leave work late. If I don't have a lot of work to do, I leave work early.
10. **the motorway** – (BrE) (AmE **freeway**) a very big road for travelling fast over long distances, often between major cities
11. **a chat with** – a conversation with (informal and friendly)
12. **telly** – television
13. **a workshop** – a room or building where tools and machines are used to repair or make things
14. **I disappear to** – I go to
15. **take up some strange habits and hobbies** – A habit is something you do regularly; a hobby is something you enjoy doing in your free time. Peter is saying that what he does in his workshop (repairing radios and clocks, etc.) is rather unusual compared to what most people do in their free time.
16. **That's the average.** – Sometimes it's later, sometimes it's earlier, but that's the usual time.

UNIT 8 Jill

This is an interview with Jill who is an operating sister at a big London hospital. Jill comes from Llanrwst, a small town in North Wales. Although she has lived away from North Wales for over 20 years, she does still have a Welsh accent. This is particularly noticeable in the way she pronounces the letter *'a'*.

A Normalisation – a typical feature of a Welsh accent

A lot of people speak Welsh in Wales as their first language. In fact Jill is bilingual, as are all her family, most of whom have remained in North Wales. A standard feature of both a North and South Welsh accent is a short 'a' sound.

Can you hear the difference between Jill's pronunciation of the following words containing *a*, and the standard, neutral pronunciation?

Short 'a' sound:

> *I go to the bathroom*
> *and I start work at 8 o'clock*
> *half an hour for lunch*
> *you can't take your lunch*
> *in the afternoon*
> *in the car*

B Normalisation – anticipating the next word

 to

Listen to tracks 155–159. There is a word missing from the end of each excerpt. Try to guess the missing word and write it down. Then listen to track 160 to check your answers. How well did you guess?

1. _____
2. _____
3. _____
4. _____
5. _____

A Putting events in order   Guess in which order Jill does the following:

(161)

_____ brushes her teeth

_____ has a cup of coffee

_____ goes downstairs

Now listen and see if you were right.

B Corrections 1

(162)

Jill talks about a typical morning. Correct the mistake in each sentence.

1. Jill lives in a flat.
2. She leaves home at 7.15.
3. She catches the W50 bus to work.
4. She starts work at 7.45.
5. She has a cup of tea at about 8.30.
6. She has an hour for lunch.

C Ticking boxes

(163)

Tick (✓) the things Jill does when she comes home.

1. ☐ She has a cup of tea.
2. ☐ She sleeps for half an hour.
3. ☐ She watches TV.
4. ☐ She reads a book.
5. ☐ She has a bath or a shower.
6. ☐ She cooks dinner.
7. ☐ She reads a newspaper.
8. ☐ She talks to her friend.

D Corrections 2

(164)

Correct the mistake in each sentence.

1. Jill goes to the pub at about 9.30pm.
2. She meets her sister in the pub.
3. She comes home about 10.30.
4. She goes to bed between 11pm and midnight.

A The present simple for talking about routines

As in the interviews with Dorothy and Peter, Jill mainly uses the present simple to talk about her routine. She also uses *will* to talk about her routine, as did Dorothy and Peter.

> *In the winter I'll have porridge . . .*
> *I generally will have a cup of coffee about eight-thirty . . .*
> *the night staff will come on at eight*
> *round about 10 o'clock we'll go up to the pub*

B To *like doing* (something)

Jill says:

*I don't **like going to bed** early.*

Here are some more examples:

> 'I like going running, but I don't like going to the gym.'
> 'I don't like walking when it's hot.'
> 'I like eating outdoors.'

A Hearing the sounds of English 1

Listen and repeat each minimal pair after the speaker.

wash/watch	bus/pus
cup/cub	pub/pup
thirty/dirty	bed/bet

B Discriminating between minimal pairs of sounds 1

Listen and underline the words you hear.

1. I must **wash/watch** this.
2. This **cup/cub** is really small.
3. I can't believe she's **thirty/dirty** already.
4. You can see the **bus/pus**.
5. The **pup/pub** is called Bentleys.
6. That's a very large **bed/bet**.

C Sentence stress

It is important that you are able to recognise stressed words in a stream of speech because these are the words that carry the speaker's meaning. Each speaker stresses the words he, or she, feels are necessary to get his, or her, message across. Underline the words you expect Jill to stress in the following extracts, then listen to check your answers.

1. when I'm working, I get up at 7 o'clock
2. I go to the bathroom and have a wash and brush my teeth.
3. And if I have time, I make myself breakfast.
4. we then do the operations during the course of the day
5. If you can, you take a break round about 10 to ten-thirty.
6. Watch a bit of television, talk to my friend, talk about my day . . .

D Recognising individual words in a stream of speech 1 – linking

When a word ends in a consonant in spoken English and the next word begins with a vowel, the end of the first word will link with the start of the second word, making it sound as if the two words are one.

Mark where you think linking will take place in the following excerpts from the interview, then listen and check your answers.

1. I get up at seven o'clock
2. have a wash and brush my teeth
3. a cup of coffee
4. the course of the day
5. we're allowed half an hour for lunch
6. my shift finishes at six o'clock

E Recognising individual words in a stream of speech 2 – dictation

Work with a partner. Listen to the excerpts from Jill's interview and write them down. Then check your answers with another pair.

1. _____
2. _____
3. _____
4. _____
5. _____
6. _____
7. _____

F Hearing the sounds of English 2

As with Exercise A, listen and repeat each minimal pair after the speaker.

teeth/tease
leave/leaf
catch/cash
work/walk
send/sent

G Discriminating between minimal pairs of sounds 2

Tick (✓) the boxes which correspond to the words you hear.

1	1	2	3	4	5
teeth					
tease					
2	1	2	3	4	5
leave					
leaf					
3	1	2	3	4	5
catch					
cash					
4	1	2	3	4	5
work					
walk					
5	1	2	3	4	5
send					
sent					

H Contractions

Contractions are common in informal spoken and written English, such as two friends chatting, emails between friends, and so on, but not in more formal English such as lectures, speeches and letters to companies.

The following contractions appear in the interview:

do not – *don't*	we are – *we're*
I am – *I'm*	we will – *we'll*
I will – *I'll*	you are – *you're*
cannot – *can't*	

Look at the following excerpts from the interview and put in the appropriate contractions. Then listen to check your answers.

1. when _____ working I get up at 7 o'clock
2. In the winter _____ have porridge . . .
3. It's round about 20 minutes . . . 15 minutes if _____ very busy.
4. And then _____ allowed half an hour for lunch.
5. Sometimes if _____ busy you _____ take your lunch.
6. and then round about 10 o'clock _____ go up to the pub
7. but I _____ like going to bed early

I Recognising individual words in a stream of speech 3 – weak forms

This gap-fill consists of excerpts from the interview and contains words which you should know, but may have problems recognising in a stream of speech.

Before you listen try to fill in the missing words. Then listen and check your answers.

1. I go to the bathroom _____ have a wash _____ brush my teeth.
2. _____ if I have time I make myself breakfast.
3. What kind _____ things do you have _____ breakfast?
4. walk _____ the bus station
5. I generally will have a cup _____ coffee about eight-thirty . . .
6. _____ then we're allowed half an hour _____ lunch.
7. So, how do you get home _____ the hospital?

J **Hearing the sounds of English 3**

As with Exercises A and F, listen and repeat each minimal pair after the speaker.

    eight/hate
    pick/Bic
    saves/safes
    bit/bid
    bed/bet

K **Discriminating between minimal pairs of sounds 3**

Tick (✓) the boxes which correspond to the words you hear.

1	1	2	3	4	5
eight					
hate					
2	1	2	3	4	5
pick					
Bic					
3	1	2	3	4	5
saves					
safes					
4	1	2	3	4	5
bit					
bid					
5	1	2	3	4	5
bed					
bet					

L Making the 'er' and 'um' sounds when pausing

When people are talking they often say *'er'* and *'um'* while they are giving themselves time to think about what they are going to say next. This can be confusing for students because *'er'* sounds like *'a'*.

What sound(s) do people make in your language when they are pausing?

Play the following excerpts and mark where Jill uses *'er'* or *'um'*, as has been done for you below.

Example:

1. Interviewer: Can you tell me about a typical day?
    Jill: Yes. **Um**, when I'm working I get up at 7 o'clock . . .

Exercise:

2. Interviewer: What kinds of things do you have for breakfast?
    Jill: Toast or cereal.
3. I leave the house at seven-thirty and walk to the bus station.
4. We then do the operations . . .
5. Then you have a 15-minute break in the afternoon.
6. I can get a bus. The W15 again. Or my friend comes to pick me up in the car.

A Extension exercise

Fill in the blanks with words you heard during Jill's interview. The words are listed in the box to help you. One of the words is used twice.

> bathroom   busy   downstairs   early   friends
> hospital   juice   late   station   walk

1. In the summer I usually _____ to work.

2. Would you like some orange _____?

3. We live near a train _____, but we go to work by bus.

4. Jan is in _____ with a broken leg.

5. I am very _____ at the moment. Can I call you back later?

6. My husband gets up very _____ in the morning – at 5 o'clock.

7. Is anyone in the _____? I want to have a shower.

8. We normally have dinner with _____ every Sunday.

9. It's _____ and I'm going to bed. I need to get up early tomorrow.

10. We have a big bathroom _____ and a shower room and toilet upstairs.

11. I don't want to _____. Can we take a taxi? I'll pay.

B The simple past of regular and irregular verbs

Put the regular and irregular verbs in brackets into the simple past. All the verbs appeared in Jill's interview.

1. I (work) _____ nearly 10 hours yesterday, so I was exhausted when I (get) _____ home.

2. We (go) _____ to Spain last month for a short holiday and it (be) _____ great. We (have) _____ a wonderful time.

3. I (make) _____ a fruit cake yesterday. Would you like a slice?

4. We (leave) _____ here at 4am and we (be) _____ in Paris at lunchtime.

5. I (walk) _____ to work yesterday because it (be) _____ such a beautiful day.

6. Sorry I'm late. I (catch) _____ the wrong bus.

7. Sarah says she (start) _____ her Christmas shopping in June! Can you believe it?

8. We (organise) _____ a surprise party for our father's 60th birthday as well and it (go) _____ really well.

9. We (send) _____ out a hundred invitations and nearly everyone (come) _____.

10. We (do) _____ a lot of sailing when we were younger, but not any more.

11. I (take) _____ this photograph on holiday in Japan.

12. Thierry (start) _____ the marathon at 8am and (finish) _____ six hours later.

13. We (save) _____ nearly £200 last month for a new car.

14. We (watch) _____ a brilliant programme on telly last night called *Miranda*. Did you see it?

15. It (be) _____ lovely to see her again, but all she (talk) _____ about was her new boyfriend, so I (get) _____ a bit bored.

16. I (meet) _____ a really nice man at a party last week. He (say) _____ he'll give me a call when he's next in New York and we can go out for a drink.

17. I (know) _____ it was a bad idea to come here on a Saturday night!

I: Can you tell me about a typical day?

J: Yes. Um, when I'm working I get up at 7 o'clock and I go to the bathroom and have a wash and brush my teeth. I go downstairs and make a cup of coffee and some fruit juice. And if I have time I make myself breakfast.

I: What kind of things do you have for breakfast?

J: Um, toast or **(1) cereal**. In the winter I'll have **(2) porridge** or something warming. Um, I leave the house at seven-thirty and er, walk to the bus station and catch the W15 bus to work, and I start work at 8 o'clock. Um, I get my **(3) theatre** ready, **(4) organise the operating list**. I generally will have a cup of coffee about eight-thirty, **(5) whilst I've sent for my first patient**. Er, we then do the operations during the course of the day. If you can, you take a break round about 10 to ten-thirty.

I: So do you have half an hour break in the morning?

J: No. It's round about 20 minutes . . . 15 minutes if you're very busy.

I: OK.

J: And then we're allowed half an hour for lunch. Sometimes if you're busy you can't take your lunch, certainly **(6) not at a conventional lunchtime**. Then you have er, a 15-minute break in the afternoon. And **(7) my shift** finishes at six o'clock.

I: Do you always finish at six?

J: No. I can finish any time from six to eight o'clock at night, really.

I: So eight o'clock's the latest?

J: Generally, because the night **(8) staff** will come on at eight **(9) and take over from you**.

I: Mmm, hmm. **(10) So how do you get home from the hospital?**

J: I can get a bus. The W15 again. Or er, my friend comes **(11) to pick me up in the car. (12) That saves a bit of time.**

I: Um, what do you do when you get home?

J: I have a cup of tea and I generally have a bath or a shower and **(13) relax**. Watch a bit of television, talk to my friend, talk about my day, my friend's day and then round about 10 o'clock we'll go up to the **(14) pub** um, and have a big talk. Meet some friends. Relax. Come home about eleven-thirty. Maybe watch a bit of television and go to bed.

I: What time do you normally go to bed?

J: I would say between midnight and one o'clock, which is quite late, I know, but I don't like going to bed early.

7. Words and Phrases

1 cereal – a breakfast food made from grain and normally eaten with milk (cornflakes, rice crispies, etc.)

2 porridge – a hot, soft breakfast food made by boiling crushed oats with milk and/or hot water (Dorothy also mentions porridge in her interview in Unit 1.)

3 (a) theatre – (full name: an operating theatre) a special room in a hospital where surgeons operate on patients

4 organise the operating list – Jill decides the order of the operations, i.e. which patient to operate on first, second, third, etc. (Dorothy also mentions a (shopping) list in Unit 1.)

5 whilst I've sent for my first patient – while Jill is waiting for someone to bring the patient to the operating theatre

6 not at a conventional lunchtime – not at a normal lunchtime, i.e. not between 12 and 2, but outside these times

7 my shift – the period of time Jill should be at work. Her shift is 8am to 6pm, but often she works later.

8 staff – workers (in this interview Jill is referring to nurses)

9 and take over from you – The night staff replace the day staff.

10 So how do you get home from the hospital? – What method of transport do you use on your journey home?

11 to pick me up – to collect me, to fetch me

12 That saves a bit of time. – (in this interview) It is quicker to go home by car than by bus.

13 (to) relax – to rest (especially after a hard day's work)

14 (a) pub – (BrE) (AmE a bar) a place where people go to relax, meet friends and drink alcoholic and non-alcoholic drinks

UNIT 9 Catherine

1. Pre-Listening Comprehension

Catherine grew up in the small market town of Llanrwst in North Wales and has lived there ever since. She is bilingual in Welsh and English and she has a strong North Welsh accent. Catherine is a pensioner but she still works as a bookkeeper. The nearest major town to Llanrwst is Llandudno.

Normalisation – questions

This exercise is designed to help you get used to Catherine's voice. Answer these questions.

1. What time does Catherine get up?
2. What does she have for breakfast?
3. What time does she start work?

Gap-fill

Catherine talks about a typical day. Before you listen, try to predict which words, or which **types** of words (nouns, adjectives, prepositions, parts of verbs, etc.) will fit in the gaps. Then listen and check your answers.

1. Catherine works in an _____ by herself.
2. She usually has a cup of _____ at 9.45 and then again at 11._____.
3. She often goes to the _____, the _____ office and then back to the office.
4. She works from nine to _____.
5. When she gets home she has a light _____ – just something on _____ or _____.
6. On Mondays and _____ Catherine and her husband go to Conway at about _____ o'clock.
7. Catherine's _____-in-law works in a _____ in Conway.
8. Catherine goes _____ at ___ o'clock on Mondays.
9. When she gets home she watches the _____ on television.
10. Catherine normally goes to her _____ house on Monday evenings.
11. She gets home at about 10._____ and her husband gets home at 10._____.

A Extension exercise

Fill in the blanks with words you heard during Catherine's interview. The words are listed in the box to help you.

> bank   egg   husband   kitchen   like
> lunch   make   mushrooms   office   only
> post   quarter   shopping   swimming   work

1. Stephen is actually my second _____. We've only been married for two years.

2. Do you want half of this pie or just a _____?

3. We've got some _____ growing in our garden, but we don't know whether we can eat them or not.

4. How would you like your _____? Fried or poached?

5. I normally drive to _____, but sometimes I walk if it's nice weather.

6. There are 10 of us in one small _____ the size of your living room.

7. I'm going to _____ some tea. Would you like a cup?

8. I need to go to the _____ to pay a cheque in, or I won't have any money next week.

9. Could you _____ this letter for me on your way to work?

10. What would you like for _____ today? Beans on toast or a pizza?

11. Do you feel _____ going for a walk? It's such a beautiful day.

12. I've _____ got two more days at work and then I'm going on holiday!

13. We need to get a bigger _____ table so that we can all sit down together when our families come over.

14. We're going _____ tomorrow. Is there anything you need?

15. I used to go _____ two or three times a week, but then I got bored with it.

B Words which go together

Put the missing verbs in the gaps in these sentences which are all based on Catherine's interview. Some of them are used more than once.

> come   do   feel   go   have   make   watch

1. I normally _____ breakfast at 10 on Sundays.
2. I _____ to work by bus.
3. We _____ a pot of coffee every morning.
4. I don't _____ like going out tonight.
5. Can we _____ home now? I'm tired.
6. I need to _____ a sit-down. I've been working in the garden for hours.
7. We usually _____ our neighbour's shopping as well because she's not very well.
8. I _____ home from the gym at seven o'clock and then have something to eat.
9. My friend and I _____ swimming on Tuesdays.
10. We don't normally _____ out on Friday evenings. We just stay at home and _____ television.

I: Can you tell me about a typical working day?

C: Yes. I get up normally between seven and quarter to eight, my husband and I. And we both have **(1) a jolly good breakfast.**

I: When you say 'a jolly good breakfast', what do you have?

C: We have mushrooms, tomatoes, bacon and egg. Um, and I go to work for nine o'clock. I walk to it – it's not far. Er, I enjoy my work very much. It's **(2) clerical work.** And I have the office to myself. Nobody comes **(3) to interrupt.** I make myself coffee **(4) whenever I feel like it,** which is usually one about quarter to ten and another about quarter past 11. **(5) I flit around** from the bank to the post office, back to the office, like that. I'm only there in the mornings till 12. I go home 12, arrive in about quarter past and my husband's always done my lunch – on the table, almost . . . which is **(6) a light lunch** – something on toast or salad, or something like that. And then we have **(7) a little sit–down.** And about 2 o'clock **(8) we make our way,** Mondays and Wednesdays, down to Conwy, where my sister-in-law works in a shop there. And we . . . because **(9) she has no transport** we take her home on a Monday, and Wednesday we do shopping for her, with her, and take her back home then. Come home again. On a Monday I go swimming five o'clock. Back home er, wa . . . watch the news and things like this. I normally go to my friend's house on a Monday because that's the only night my husband goes out. And that's it. And I'm home about half-past 10 and my husband's home about quarter to 11. We watch something on television we've either **(10) taped** or something and then bed. And that's it.

5. Words and Phrases

1 **a jolly good breakfast** – (old-fashioned) a very nice breakfast
2 **clerical work** – work done in an office
3 **to interrupt** – to stop someone doing something for a short period, as in 'Please don't interrupt me when I'm talking!'
4 **whenever I feel like it** – whenever I want
5 **I flit around** – I walk quickly from place to place
6 **a light lunch** – not a big lunch
7 **a little sit–down** – a short period of sitting to rest and relax
8 **we make our way** – we go
9 **she has no transport** – she doesn't have a car
10 **taped** – recorded on video

UNIT **10** Danny

1. Pre-Listening Comprehension

We heard Danny talking about his family in Unit 5. Danny is a student at Nottingham University. He spent a year in Dover on a placement as part of his studies. Danny comes from a small market town near Cambridge.

Normalisation – questions

This exercise is designed to help you get used to Danny's voice. Listen and answer the following questions.

1. What hours does Danny often work?
2. What time does he usually get up?
3. What does he have for breakfast?
4. How long does it take him to walk to work?

2. Listening Comprehension

Corrections

Correct the mistake in each sentence.

1. If it's raining Danny takes a bus to work.

   _____

2. The first customer arrives at 11.15.

   _____

3. He is a Welshman called Alan.

   _____

4. Danny often has a bag of sweets for lunch.

   _____

5. Sometimes Nick gives Danny a lift home after work.

   _____

6. When he gets home, Danny has a sleep.

   _____

7. He relaxes in the evenings by watching a film or listening to music on his iPod.

   _____

8. Sometimes Danny cooks some chicken with rice or potatoes.

   _____

9. Danny is staying with friends at the moment.

   _____

10. He is living in Spruce Hills Street.

    _____

11. His road is near the Town Hall and the church.

    _____

A Extension exercise   Fill in the blanks with words you heard during Danny's interview.
The words are listed in the box to help you.

> bell   cab   couple   customer   feel
> lift   meal   peckish   sauce   save   shift
> tide   toast   walk   weather   work

1.   I'm trying to _____ money at the moment because I'm going on
     holiday next month.

2.   We're not allowed to make personal calls at _____.

3.   Do you want _____ or bread and butter?

4.   Can you wait a _____ of minutes? I just want to change my shoes.

5.   We usually go for a long _____ after Sunday lunch if the
     _____ is OK.

6.   I'm going to get a _____ home. It's too cold to wait for a bus.

7.   We opened the shop at nine and our first _____ came in at two
     minutes past.

8.   Sorry, I didn't hear the _____. I had my music on too loud.

9.   Would you like a _____ home as it's raining? My car's just round
     the corner.

10. Would you like to come round for a _____ sometime? I'm a really
     good cook.

11. I don't _____ like watching television. Can we go out?

12. We normally have mint _____ with lamb, but the children hate it.

13. I'm feeling a bit _____. Have we got anything to eat? I need
     something to _____ me over until dinner.

14. Whenever I do a night _____ then I get the next day off.

B Transformations

Change the word in each bracket which Danny used in his interview to form a word which fits the gap.

1. The children are really (exciting) _____ about Christmas.

2. I haven't got much money in my (save) _____ account at the moment.

3. Is it going to (raining) _____ tomorrow?

4. Why don't you sit over here? It's (nice) _____ in the sunshine?

5. The telephone (rings) _____ for ages before he answered it.

6. Why don't you have a break? I think you're (work) _____ too hard.

7. We had a great time in Spain. It was the most (relax) _____ holiday we've ever had.

8. Why is it boys never wash their necks (proper) _____?

9. I'm not (eat) _____ eggs at the moment because I'm on a low cholesterol diet.

10. What is the main (ingredients) _____ in béchamel sauce?

I: Can you tell me about a typical day when you're working?

D: A typical day here?

I: Yeah.

D: It's not very **(1) exciting** (*laughs*) because **(2) basically** I'm trying to save my money for when I go back to university. So I don't go out at the moment, I'm just putting the money in the bank.

I: OK.

D: But say I'm at work . . . er, take **(3) for instance** I'm working 11 till 7.

I: Mmm. In **(4) the bar.**

D: In the bar.

I: OK.

D: I will normally get up at about 10 o'clock. Have a shower, have a couple of slices of toast and a cup of tea and er, walk down. It's only about a 10-minute walk. But if the weather's (*laughs*) if the weather's nice then it's quite a nice walk. If it's raining I'll probably just get **(5) a cab.**

I: Um, what . . . 'cos you open at 11, is it?

D: 11 o'clock.

I: Yeah. What time does the first customer arrive?

D: 11 o'clock.

I: 11 o'clock! (*laughs*) Is there a line of them, or just . . .

D: And it's always Alan. Alan is er, Scottish. He comes in every morning and if we're not open **(6) at 11 on the dot,** he rings the bell.

I: Goodness!

D: (*laughs*) Yeah, he's always in.

I: OK. Um, do you, do you have **(7) a lunch break?**

D: No! (*laughs*)

I: You work straight through?

D: I should, I should . . .

I: But . . .

D: But **(8) I normally just grab a bag of crisps** or something halfway through the day, **(9) once I get peckish.**

I: Mmm, hmm. So the minute you finish here, what do you do? What's the first thing you do?

D: The minute I finish here?

I: Yeah.

D: Leave! (*laughs*)

I: So you walk out the door. Do you get a cab home? Or bus, or?

D: I normally walk.

I: Right.

D: But if um, if Mick's here **(10) he gives me a lift.** So it's OK that way. Get in and have a shower (*laughs*) and then er, I normally just try and relax in the evenings.

I: Mmm. How do you do that?

D: Well, I've got my um, like I say, I don't go out at the moment 'cos I'm trying to save my money, so I might just put a film on or . . .

I: Mmm. What, a DVD or something?

D: A DVD or a video. And er, I've got my PC in my . . . here at the moment.

I: Mmm.

D: So maybe just listen to some music I've got on there.

I: Right. When do you eat? 'Cos so far you haven't had **(11) a proper meal** all day.

D: I had some toast for breakfast (*laughs*) . . .

I: OK.

D: . . . and a cup of tea.

I: Yeah. Bag of crisps for lunch.

D: A bag of crisps for lunch, but maybe I'll get in and . . . **(12) I don't normally feel like eating after working.** I don't know why. But if I do go back home and I'm on the day shift and I go back then I might do myself something to eat, but I normally just do maybe some chicken with some rice or pasta and some sauce. It won't be anything particularly big.

I: Mmm.

D: It'll just be something **(13) to tide me over,** you know, 'cos . . .

I: Till the next day.

D: Till the next day. Yeah.

I: Do you make your own sauce for the chicken?

D: Not normally. I can! But (*laughs*) you have to have **(14) the right ingredients.**

I: OK. Where are you living at the moment?

D: I'm liv . . . staying with my dad at the moment.

I: Oh, right.

D: In um, it's a road called Spruce Hills Road.

I: Oh, yeah.

D: It's near the Town Hall.

I: Mmm.

D: And the college, near the college.

I: Right.

1 **exciting** – (in this interview) interesting
2 **basically** – the most important thing is
3 **for instance** – for example
4 **the bar** – another word for a pub
5 **a cab** – a taxi
6 **at 11 on the dot** – at exactly 11 o'clock
7 **a lunch break** – time away from work to have lunch
8 **I normally just grab a bag of crisps** – I usually just take a bag of crisps and eat them quickly (crisps are thin, deep-fried slices of potato)
9 **once I get peckish** – when I become a little bit hungry
10 **he gives me a lift** – he takes me home in his car
11 **a proper meal** – a real meal (i.e. not just a snack like crisps)
12 **I don't normally feel like eating after working.** – I don't usually want to eat after work.
13 **to tide me over** – to stop me feeling hungry until the next day or to keep me going until the next day
14 **the right ingredients** – all the things you need to cook a sauce, casserole, curry, etc.

A Place I Know Well

UNIT **11** Danny

We heard Danny talking in Unit 5 and Unit 10. In this unit he talks about Dover, where he spent a year on a placement as part of his studies. Danny comes from a small market town near Cambridge.

Normalisation

Tick (✓) the correct box.

1. Danny lived in Dover in his **first** ☐ **second** ☐ **third** ☐ year at university.

2. Danny says Dover is a very **small** ☐ **smelly** ☐ **sunny** ☐ place.

3. The two big ferry companies in Dover are **Sea France and B&O Ferries** ☐ **Sea France and P&O Ferries** ☐ **Sea French and P&O Ferries** ☐.

Multiple Choice

Tick (✓) the correct box.

1. You can see the sights of Dover with **a tour boat** ☐ **a tour bus** ☐.

2. Danny lived in a **flat** ☐ **hostel** ☐ **hotel** ☐ in Dover.

3. He lived near **the castle** ☐ **the beach** ☐ **the cliffs** ☐.

4. Danny says the sea was **grey** ☐ **blue** ☐ **green** ☐.

5. The beach was **sandy** ☐ **stony** ☐.

6. Halfway up the White Cliffs of Dover there seem to be **trees** ☐ **caves** ☐ **cottages** ☐.

7. Danny never did a tour of Dover because **he didn't have enough time** ☐ **he didn't have enough money** ☐.

8. When Danny lived in Dover he sometimes went to **Calais** ☐ **Carlisle** ☐ **Paris** ☐.

9. Danny likes the **shops** ☐ **restaurants** ☐ **bars** ☐ in the French town.

Dover

A *used to* (do something) for past habit

The interviewer begins the interview by saying:

Now you used to live in Dover, I think?

We use *used to* + *infinitive* to talk about things that we did regularly in the past or states that went on for some time in the past. We often use *used to* to talk about something we did when we were younger, but that we don't do any more. Look at these examples:

'I used to walk two miles to school every day.'
'All the kids used to play in the street.'
'I used to wear trainers to work in my last job.'

B *must have been* for assumptions

When the interviewer hears that Danny's hotel was near the beach she says:

That must have been nice.

We use *must have* + past participle when we talk about something in the past which we assume was true. In this case the interviewer is sure that it was nice for Danny to stay in a hotel near the sea. Later the interviewer asks how white the White Cliffs of Dover are. Danny says:

You must have seen pictures.

In this case Danny is sure that the interviewer has, at some time in her life, seen pictures of the cliffs and therefore knows that they are really white.

C Introduction to the present perfect simple

The interviewer says:

I've never been to Dover.

This usage of the present perfect simple is very common when people are meeting for the first time and getting to know each other.

D *'cos* instead of *because* in spoken English

Both the interviewer and Danny use *'cos* instead of *because*. This is a common feature of fast spoken English.

Interviewer: *In your third year 'cos, 'cos you're a student.*
Danny: *It portrays that it is nice, 'cos you have the tour bus that goes round to see the sights of Dover.*

E The glottal stop

The glottal stop occurs when the speaker constricts his or her throat and blocks the air stream completely. This results in the speaker not pronouncing fully the –t sound at the end of words such as *got* or *lot*, or the –t– sounds in words such as *bottle* or *kettle*. This is a common feature of many British accents, and is used particularly by younger people. Notice how Danny uses a glottal stop in the following excerpts:

no͟t a lo͟t of people	*I never go͟t a chance*
*It portrays **that it** is nice.*	*It was **quite** expensive.*
***Bu͟t** it was a nice view.*	***Didn't ge͟t** any further than Calais.*
*very **whi͟te***	

F Falling intonation for statements

In British English the voice generally falls at the end of the statement. This signals that the speaker has finished making a point. It also signals that the other person can now say something without fear of interrupting the speaker. Listen to Danny making the following statements and pay attention to where his voice begins to fall:

It's mainly just a harbour town.

The sea's surprisingly blue, for England.

You must have seen pictures.

They are really white.

I never did the tour.

I never got a chance.

Didn't get any further than Calais.

G Simplification

When we speak quickly a process known as 'simplification' occurs. The speaker cuts corners and doesn't articulate words clearly. This makes it difficult for you to recognise words even if you know them already. Listen to the following words in isolation:

comfortable   ***supposed***

How has the pronunciation of these words changed in a stream of speech?

So it wasn't too <u>comfortable</u>.
But Calais's <u>supposed</u> to be a nice place.

A Linking

Linking occurs when the end of one word runs_into the start_of the next word. It is very common in informal spoken English, but less so in more formal English, such as speeches or lectures.

The most common linking occurs between the letter –s at the end of a word when the next word begins with a vowel, as in these excerpts from the interview:

> Third year **was_in** Dover.
> But it **was_a** nice view.

However, linking also occurs with other sounds. Mark where linking occurs in these excerpts from the interview.

1. Can you tell me a bit about the town?
2. two big main companies: Sea France and P&O ferries
3. that's about it
4. The sea's surprisingly blue, for England.
5. But that's about all you can do . . .
6. There are parts of it that are nice.
7. Has it got a beach there?
8. Which is a bonus.

Now read these phrases and sentences aloud and remember to link words.

B Hearing the sounds of English 1

Listen and repeat each minimal pair after the speaker.

live/leave	white/right
think/sink	side/sight
town/down	beach/peach
harbour/arbour	

C Discriminating between minimal pairs of sounds 1

Listen and underline which word you hear.

1. I think we should **leave/live** here.
2. I can see you're **sinking/thinking**.
3. I can see **he's down/his town**.
4. What a beautiful **arbour/harbour**!
5. Isn't that **right/white**?
6. Which **side/sight** are you talking about?
7. What a wonderful **beach/peach**!

D Contractions

Contractions are common in informal spoken and written English, such as two friends chatting, emails between friends, and so on, but not in more formal English such as lectures, speeches and letters to companies.

Look at the following excerpts from the interview and put in the contracted forms of the underlined words. Then listen to find out if you were correct.

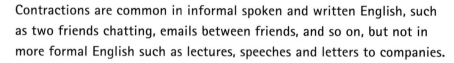

Example: I have never been to Dover. **I've**

1. It is mainly just a harbour town. _____
2. there are not many to see _____
3. that is about it _____
4. it was not sand _____
5. but you do not know if they are still cave entrances _____/_____
6. unless you have got transport _____

E Sentence stress

Stressed words are the most important in spoken English because they carry the most meaning. Which words are stressed in the following extracts?

1. Now you used to live in Dover, I think?
2. It's mainly just a harbour town . . .
3. people go there to cross the Channel to France
4. you have the tour bus that goes round to see the sights of Dover
5. the castle's the main attraction
6. The view was nice.
7. But the beach was nothing special because it wasn't sand. It was stones.
8. There are parts of it that are nice.

F Recognising individual words in a stream of speech

Work with a partner. Listen to the excerpts from Danny's interview and write them down. Then check your answers with another pair.

1. _____
2. _____
3. _____
4. _____
5. _____

G Hearing the sounds of English 2

As with Exercise B, listen and repeat each minimal pair after the speaker.

right/light	been/bin
main/man	still/steel
bus/buzz	while/whirl
view/phew	

H Discriminating between minimal pairs of sounds 2

Tick (✓) the boxes which correspond to the words you hear.

1	1	2	3	4	5
right					
light					
2	1	2	3	4	5
main					
man					
3	1	2	3	4	5
bus					
buzz					
4	1	2	3	4	5
view					
phew					
5	1	2	3	4	5
been					
bin					
6	1	2	3	4	5
still					
steel					
7	1	2	3	4	5
while					
whirl					

I Weak forms

The pronunciation of *to*, *for* and *of* often changes to a weaker form in spoken English which is not as clear.

Try to fill in the missing words in these excerpts and then listen to check your answers. How does the pronunciation of *to*, *for* and *of* change in informal spoken English?

1. I've never been _____ Dover.
2. not a lot _____ people there
3. basically people go there _____ cross the Channel
4. The sea's surprisingly blue, _____ England.
5. Now they talk about the White Cliffs _____ Dover.
6. A lot _____ restaurants.
7. You have the tour bus that goes round _____ see the sights _____ Dover.
8. If you just go over _____ the day, Calais's about as far as you can go.

J Gap–fill – elision

When speaking quickly in English, people often miss out individual sounds at the ends of words — a process known as elision. For example, a speaker will say *las' night* instead of *last night*, *jus' got here* instead of *just got here*, or *trie' to* instead of *tried to*.

Try to fill in the missing words in these extracts, all of which have been affected by elision.

1. Now you _____ _____ live in Dover, I think.
2. You have the tour bus that _____ _____ to see the sights of Dover.
3. It _____ _____ you round the, round the beach area . . .
4. If you _____ _____ over for the day, Calais's about as far as you can go.

5. Further Language Development

A Extension exercise

Fill in the blanks with words you heard during Danny's interview.

> beach   companies   expensive   ferry   harbour
> population   sea   stones   student   used   view

1. I _____ to like sugar in my tea when I was young, but now I find it too sweet.

2. What is the _____ of London? Is it eight million?

3. The next _____ to Sweden leaves in half an hour.

4. There is a very nice sandy _____ in Bournemouth which is wonderful for young children to play on.

5. I have a wonderful _____ of the sea from my office window.

6. These restaurants are all very _____. Shall we go to a café instead?

7. My brother is a _____ at this college.

8. When the weather is very bad, most ships stay in the _____.

9. I've got interviews next week with two different _____ — one in Bristol and one in Birmingham.

10. I don't like swimming in the _____ in this country because it's too cold. I prefer a swimming pool.

11. These _____ hurt your feet, don't they? I wish I'd worn better shoes, but I didn't know we were going for a walk on the beach.

B Introduction to the present perfect simple

We use the present perfect simple to talk about things that have, or haven't happened during a period of time leading up the present. To form the present perfect simple we use the verb *to have* + past participle.

Put the verbs in brackets into the present perfect simple.

1. I (live) _____ here since 2005.

2. Peter (lose) _____ 10 kilos since he started that diet.

3. Sorry, I (use) _____ all the milk.

4. We (buy) _____ a new car!

5. I (finish) _____ my homework at last.

6. I (post) _____ your letter.

7. Phil and Sam (move) _____ to New York.

8. Oh no! Yuko (leave) _____ her mobile phone behind.

9. I (decide) _____ to get a new job.

10. Is it true you (stop) _____ eating meat?

C Prepositions

Put the correct prepositions in the gaps. Some of them are used more than once.

> about   for   in   of   on   to

1. I used to live _____ Chicago, but last year I moved _____ New York.

2. Tell me all _____ your holiday!

3. I can't come out tonight. I've got a lot _____ work to do.

4. My idea of a perfect holiday is lying _____ a beach with a good book.

5. It gets very cold here _____ the winter.

6. She's very grown-up _____ her age.

7. When we looked out of our window we saw the car was covered _____ snow.

8. Which part _____ Bulgaria do you come from?

9. We're going _____ Russia next month _____ a wedding.

10. Could you sit _____ the other side _____ Rachel?

D Transformations

Change the word in each bracket which Danny used in his interview to form a word which fits the gap.

1. What subject are you (student) _____ at university?

2. How much does it cost to go from Dover to Calais by (ferries) _____?

3. I've got a wonderful (surprisingly) _____ for your birthday!

4. Our hotel was right next to a beautiful (sand) _____ beach.

5. I don't like going to London in the summer because it's always full of (tour) _____.

I: OK. Now you used to live in Dover, I think?

D: I did **(1) a placement** in Dover in my third year.

I: In your third year 'cos, 'cos you're a student.

D: That's right.

I: Third year was in Dover. I've never been to Dover. Can you tell me a bit about the town?

D: It's mainly just **(2) a harbour town**, with . . .

I: Right. So lots of ships . . . coming in.

D: . . . what you'd expect from a harbour town. Very small, not a lot of people there, small **(3) population**, and, like you said, **(4) basically** people go there to cross **(5) the Channel** to France.

I: OK. So they have big **(6) ferries** there?

D: Big ferries, **(7) hovercraft**, two big main companies: Sea France and P&O Ferries.

I: Um, is the town nice?

D: No.

I: No. (*laughs*)

D: **(8) It portrays that it is nice**, 'cos you have **(9) the tour bus** that goes round to see **(10) the sights** of Dover, but there aren't many to see.

I: What are they, then?

D: Well, **(11) the castle's the main attraction. (12) The cliffs, (13) obviously** and um . . . that's about it. It just takes you round the, round the **(14) beach** area um, which is where my hotel was, on the beach area.

I: Oh, that must have been nice.

D: The **(15) view** was nice. (*laughs*)

I: Mmm, hmm.

D: But not in the winter.

I: Right, but, but . . . sort of like in the summer, was the sea blue and . . .?

D: The sea's **(16) surprisingly blue**, for England.

I: Mmm, hmm. Right.

D: But the beach was nothing special because it wasn't **(17) sand**. It was **(18) stones**.

I: Right.

D: So it wasn't too comfortable.

I: Mmm, hmm.

D: But it was a nice view.

I: Now they talk about the White Cliffs of Dover. Are they really white?

D: Very white. You must have seen pictures.

I: I've seen pictures, yeah. But I've, I've never been to Dover.

D: They are really white. Some are covered in **(19) forestry**, but mostly white.

I: What – trees and **(20) bushes** and . . .

D: Trees and bushes and you still have the odd, um, the odd . . . it's sort of . . . it's hard to explain. You see kind of **(21) cave** entrances halfway up the cliff, but you don't know if they're still cave entrances. I think they might be past, part of the castle, the und . . . underneath.

I: Sort of **(22) tunnels**.

D: Tunnels.

I: **(23) To store things.**

D: I've never been. I never did the tour.

I: OK.

D: **(24) I never got a chance**. It was quite expensive. But yeah, I think they're the tunnels of the castle.

I: Right. OK. Um, did you ever go to France while you were living in Dover?

D: I did. Didn't get any further than Calais.

I: Mmm.

D: But that's about all you can do is . . . unless you've got **(25) transport**, go over with transport. If you just go over for the day, Calais's about as far as you can go.

I: **(26) But Calais's supposed to be a nice place.**

D: There are parts of it that are nice. A lot of restaurants. Um, but it's mainly just a small French harbour town, like Dover is, on the other side of the water.

I: Has it got a beach there?

D: It does . . . with sand.

I: Oh, right.

D: (*laughs*) Which is **(27) a bonus**.

1 **a placement** – Business Studies students often spend part of their studies working for a company which may be some distance away from their university.

2 **a harbour town** – a town near an area of water next to the coast often protected from the sea by a thick wall, where ships and boats can dock

3 **population** – the number of people living in a country or place, e.g. What's the population of New York City?

4 **basically** – the most important thing is that . . .

5 **the Channel** – (the English Channel) the area of water separating England from France

6 **ferries** (plural) **a ferry**– A ferry is a boat used to transport passengers and vehicles across water as a regular service.

7 **(a) hovercraft** – a vehicle which goes over water or land on a cushion of air

8 **It portrays that it is nice** – (unusual usage) It gives the impression that it is nice.

9 **the tour bus** – a bus which takes people to the most interesting parts of the town

10 **the sights** (plural) – the places of interest, especially to visitors

11 **the castle's the main attraction** – the reason most people visit Dover is to see the castle – the large old stone building on top of the cliffs

12 **The cliffs** (plural) – A cliff is a high area of rock or chalk with very steep sides, often on the coast.

13 **obviously** – it's easy to understand why

14 **(a) beach** – an area of sand or small stones beside the sea

15 **(a) view** – what you can see from a particular place

16 **surprisingly blue** – unexpectedly blue, more blue than you would think

17 **sand** – very small grains of rock found on beaches or in deserts such as the Sahara

18 **stones** (plural) **a stone** – small pieces of rock

19 **forestry** – (unusual usage) The real meaning of forestry is planting and looking after trees. Danny means forests – a forest is a large area of land with trees.

20 **bushes** (plural) – A bush is a plant smaller than a tree with lots of small, thin branches.

21 **(a) cave** – a large hole in the side of a hill, cliff or mountain

22 **tunnels** (plural) **a tunnel**– A tunnel is a long passage through the earth, often made by people.

23 **To store things.** – To put or keep things in a special place for future use.

24 **I never got a chance.** – I never had the opportunity to do this.

25 **transport** – (in this case) if you have your own car or motorbike

26 **But Calais's supposed to be a nice place.** – But people say Calais is a nice place.

27 **a bonus** – (in this case) a pleasant extra thing

UNIT **12** Catherine

1. Pre-Listening Comprehension

We heard Catherine talking about her daily routine in Unit 9. Catherine grew up in the small market town of Llanrwst in North Wales and has lived there ever since. She is bilingual in Welsh and English and she has a strong North Welsh accent. Catherine is a pensioner but she still works as a bookkeeper. The nearest major town to Llanrwst is Llandudno.

A Welsh pronunciation

If a Welsh word begins with *ll*, as in the town *Llanrwst*, it is pronounced by placing the tongue loosely across the top of the mouth and breathing out through your cheeks.

However, people outside Wales usually ignore this and pronounce the double *l* as a single *l*. Try to say *Llanelli*.

In Welsh the letter *w* in a word is pronounced as the letter *u*, so Llanrwst is actually pronounced 'Llanroost'.

In Welsh the letter *u* is pronounced as the letter *i*, so Llandudno is actually pronounced 'Llandidno' by Welsh people.

The letter *y* in Welsh is pronounced as the letter *u*, so the word for Wales – Cymru – is actually pronounced 'Cumree'.

B Normalisation – anticipating the next word

 to
 to

Listen to tracks 214–218. There is a word missing from the end of each excerpt. Try to guess the missing word and write it down. Then listen to tracks 219–223 to check your answers. How well did you guess?

1. _____

2. _____

3. _____

4. _____

5. _____

A Corrections 1

Catherine talks about the small town of Llanrwst. Correct the mistake in each sentence.

1. Llanrwst is a large market town.

2. The bridge was built by Inigo James.

3. He built the bridge in 1638.

4. Llanrwst has lots of visitors in winter.

5. The café in the cottage looks beautiful in the spring.

6. The cricket team play on Sundays.

7. There are mountains on one side of the valley and trees on the other.

B Gap-fill

Catherine talks about going down to the nearest major town, Llandudno.

Before you listen, try to predict which words, or which types of words (nouns, adjectives, prepositions, parts of verbs, etc.) will fit in the gaps. Then listen and check your answers.

1. Catherine can see _____ from the back of her house.
2. There are _____ each side of the road from Llanrwst to Llandudno.
3. The road follows the _____ down to the sea.
4. There are beautiful _____ along the promenade in Llandudno.
5. Catherine goes to Llandudno at least once a _____.

C Questions

Catherine talks about a typical day out in Llandudno. Listen and answer the questions.

1. Which supermarket does Catherine go to?
2. Who does she take with her?
3. What day do they usually go to Llandudno?
4. What is *The Cottage Loaf*?
5. What does Catherine's friend love buying?
6. What time does Catherine usually come home from her day in Llandudno?

D Corrections 2

Catherine talks about housework and a typical Saturday. Correct the mistake in each sentence.

1. Catherine's husband hates doing the washing.
2. Catherine does the ironing on Monday mornings.
3. On Saturdays she meets her friends for lunch.
4. They spend two hours together.

A **The present simple**   Catherine uses the present simple when she talks about things which happen regularly, as in the following examples:

> they _play_ cricket there
> Lots of people _go_ and _watch_ it on a Saturday afternoon.
> I _do_ my shopping in Asda there.
> We _do_ our shopping in Asda.
> we _meet_ in a little old-fashioned café . . .

B _Used to_ (do something) for past habit   As with Danny in Unit 1, Catherine uses _used to_ when she talks about the old tennis courts.

> There used to be tennis courts there . . .

Here are some more examples of this usage:

> 'There used to be a field here, but now it's a car park.'
> 'I'm sure there used to be a tree here.'
> 'This room used to be a bedroom but now I use it as my office.'

C **The simple past**   Catherine uses the simple past passive when she talks about the bridge over the River Conway in Llanrwst.

> and an old bridge which _was built_ by Inigo Jones in 1636

To form the simple past passive we use the simple past of the verb _to be_ and add the past participle. Here are some more examples:

> 'The Taj Mahal _was built_ between 1630 and 1653.'
> 'The Lord of the Rings movies _were filmed_ in New Zealand.'
> 'This photo of me _was taken_ in 1997.'

D *It is* and *There are*

When we are talking about something for the first time we generally say *There is . . .*, whereas when we are giving details about something we have already referred to we say *It is . . ..*

Look at these examples from the interview where Catherine mentions things in Llanrwst for the first time:

There's a river flowing through it . . .
And there's a putting place on the um, the other side of the river.
There's a nice bowling green there.

Now look at these examples where Catherine is giving details about Llanrwst:

Well, it's a little market town. It's a pretty little town.
Yes, it's a very pleasant place to live.

Later she talks about her husband doing the washing. She says:

And it's usually dry and folded by the time I get home.

4. Further Listening Practice

A Sentence stress

 to

Speakers stress the words they feel are important to convey their meaning. Which words are stressed in the following extracts?

1. It's a pretty little town.
2. it has lots of visitors in summer
3. beautiful colour in the autumn
4. There's a nice bowling green there.
5. Yes, it's a very pleasant place to live.
6. we have a day out on a Friday, usually
7. We do our shopping in Asda.

B Hearing the sounds of English 1

Listen and repeat each minimal pair after the speaker.

river/liver	clothes/crows
watch/wash	washing/watching
back/pack	dry/try
shopping/chopping	

C Discriminating between minimal pairs of sounds 1

Listen and underline which word you hear.

1. This **river/liver** is wonderful!
2. You need a **watch/wash**.
3. My **back/pack** is hurting.
4. You do the **shopping/chopping** and I'll do the cooking.
5. What a lot of **clothes/crows**!
6. He's always **washing/watching** his car.
7. You must **dry/try** this.

D Weak forms

As with Danny's interview, the pronunciation of *to*, *for*, *from* and *of* has changed to a weaker form which is not as clear. Try to fill in the missing words in these excerpts and then listen to check your answers.

How has the pronunciation of *to*, *for*, *from* and *of* changed?

1. What kind _____ place is it?
2. So can you see mountains _____ your house?
3. So Llandudno is next _____ the sea, then . . .
4. Lots _____ people go and watch it on a Saturday afternoon.
5. What time do you come home _____ a day in Llandudno?
6. Then I go out and meet a couple of my friends _____ coffee.

E Hearing the sounds of English 2

As with Exercise B, listen and repeat each minimal pair after the speaker.

town/down   very/ferry
old/hold   next/nest
green/grin   called/cold
back/pack

F Discriminating between minimal pairs of sounds 2

Tick (✓) the boxes which correspond to the words you hear.

1	1	2	3	4	5
town					
down					

2	1	2	3	4	5
old					
hold					

3	1	2	3	4	5
green					
grin					

4	1	2	3	4	5
back					
pack					

5	1	2	3	4	5
very					
ferry					

6	1	2	3	4	5
next					
nest					

7	1	2	3	4	5
called					
cold					

G 'um' for pauses

When people are talking they often say *'um'* while they are giving themselves time to think about what they are going to say next. What sounds do you make in your own language when you are pausing?

Listen and mark where Catherine uses *'um'* in the following excerpts:

1. And it has lots of visitors in summer.
2. And there's a putting place on the the other side of the river.
3. and they play cricket there . . .
4. we meet in a little old-fashioned café called the Hên Aelwyd . . . only 11 till 12.

H Recognising individual words in a stream of speech – dictation

 to

Work with a partner. Listen to the excerpts from Catherine's interview and write them down. Then check your answers with another pair.

1. _____ .

2. _____ .

3. _____ . . .

4. _____ .

5. _____ ?

6. _____ ?

7. _____ ?

8. _____ .

9. _____ .

I Hearing the sounds of English 3

As with Exercises B and E, listen and repeat each minimal pair after the speaker.

built/build   meet/mitt
team/Tim   side/sight
live/leave   quite/quiet
first/thirst

Llanrwst

J Discriminating between minimal pairs of sounds 3

Tick (✓) the boxes which correspond to the words you hear.

1	1	2	3	4	5
built					
build					
2	1	2	3	4	5
team					
Tim					
3	1	2	3	4	5
live					
leave					
4	1	2	3	4	5
first					
thirst					
5	1	2	3	4	5
meet					
mitt					
6	1	2	3	4	5
side					
sight					
7	1	2	3	4	5
quite					
quiet					

K Linking

As with Danny's interview there are numerous examples of linking in this interview.

Linking occurs when the end of one word runs_into the start_of the

next word. It is very common in informal spoken English, but less so in more formal English, such as speeches or lectures.

The most common linking occurs between the letter *-s* at the end of a word when the next word begins with a vowel, as in these excerpts from the interview. However, linking also occurs with other sounds.

Mark where linking occurs in these excerpts from the interview.

1. Well, it's a little market town.

2. It's a pretty little town.

3. There's a river flowing through it . . .

4. it has lots of visitors in summer

5. There's a nice bowling green there.

6. Round the back of it, yes, easily.

7. 'Queen of Resorts of North Wales', they reckon.

8. Beautiful hotels along the promenade . . .

9. Once a week at least, yes.

10. And it's usually dry and folded by the time I get home.

L Gap-fill – elision

As we heard in Danny's interview, when speaking quickly in English, people often miss out individual sounds at the ends of words — a process known as elision. For example, a speaker will say *las' night* instead of *last night*, *jus' got here* instead of *just got here*, or *trie' to* instead of *tried to*.

Fill in the missing words in these extracts, all of which have been affected by elision.

1. Well, it's a little _____ _____.

2. and an _____ _____

3. There _____ _____ be tennis courts there . . .

4. _____ the back of it, yes, easily

5. Yes, it's a very _____ place to live.

6. So Llandudno is _____ _____ the sea, then . . .

7. _____ my friend

8. We'll have gone _____ _____ in the morning.

A Extension exercise Fill in the blanks with words you heard during Catherine's interview.

> been   colour   cottage   dry   field   hotels
> husband   living   mountains   river   sea
> shopping   tennis   tiny   town   watch

1. A place which is bigger than a village, but smaller than a city is called a_____.

2. The best place to go fishing in this _____ is near the old bridge.

3. My sister lives in a tiny old _____ in the country.

4. What _____ is your new car?

5. In the summer I play _____ and in the winter I play squash.

6. Lots of people _____ television before they go to work.

7. The highest _____ in Norway always have snow on them, even in summer.

8. There is a big _____ behind my friend's house which is full of sheep.

9. The River Conway flows into the _____ at Llandudno.

10. They say _____ in New York are very expensive. Even a cheap one costs at least $100 a night.

11. Your feet are _____! Mine are twice as big as yours!

12. My _____ and I share the housework.

13. This plant is very _____. Shall I give it some water?

14. I've never _____ to Turkey.

15. We always go _____ on Thursdays.

16. How long have you been _____ in this flat?

B Gap-fill

This is a revision exercise. You will probably be able to complete it correctly, even without hearing the extract again. The missing words are listed in the box. One of the words is used twice.

Try to predict the missing words before you listen. Then listen and check your answers.

> called   first   friends   home   husband   loves
> lunch   our   out   past   street   time   washing

Catherine: We do **(1)** _____ shopping in Asda. Park there. Go up town. Park there again. Have **(2)** _____ in a little . . . little tiny pub **(3)** _____ the Cottage Loaf. And then we do the shopping at the main **(4)** _____, for my friend **(5)** _____ to shop for clothes and things. (*laughs*)

Interviewer: What time do you come **(6)** _____ from a day in Llandudno?

Catherine: Oh, about **(7)** half-_____ four. We'll have gone about 10 in the morning. And my poor **(8)** _____ is home doing the **(9)** _____, every week, which he **(10)** _____. And it's usually dry and folded by the **(11)** _____ I get home.

Interviewer: Does your husband do the ironing as well?

Catherine: No, no, no. I do that **(12)** _____ thing on a Saturday morning. Then I go **(13)** _____ and meet a couple of my **(14)** _____ for coffee.

C The present simple and present continuous

We generally use the present simple to talk about things that happen regularly, as in this example from Catherine's interview:

We <u>do</u> our shopping in Asda.

We generally use the present continuous to talk about things we are doing at the moment, as in this example:

'It's my birthday and I <u>am having</u> a wonderful day.'

Put the verbs in brackets into either the present simple or the present continuous, as appropriate.

1. Can you speak a bit louder? Adrian (cut) _____ the grass and I can't hear you very well.
2. Normally I (do) _____ all the cooking at the weekend.
3. My sister (study) _____ to be a lawyer.
4. We (go) _____ to Canada at least twice a year.
5. I usually (start) _____ work at nine, but sometimes I (go) _____ in earlier.
6. Sarah (play) _____ in the garden. Shall I get her for you?
7. This train (go) _____ really slowly. I'm sure we're going to be late.

D Transformations

Change the word in each bracket which Catherine used in her interview to form a word which fits the gap.

1. This is the (pretty) _____ village I've ever seen.
2. Who is the (old) _____ of your brothers and sisters?
3. This (built) _____ wasn't here when I was a girl.
4. Don't forget to (covered) _____ the fish with milk before cooking.
5. I drew the picture and then Daisy (colour) _____ it in. Isn't it great?
6. Who's your favourite football (play) _____?
7. I'm (watch) _____ a really interesting programme. Can I call you back?
8. I think you'll find it's (easily) _____ to open if you take the plastic off.
9. The best (shopping) _____ are at the other end of High Street.
10. I like her new boyfriend. He's much (friend) _____ than her last one.
11. Can you seek a (park) _____ space anywhere?

I: Can you um, tell me about Llanrwst? What kind of place is it?

C: Well, it's a little **(1) market town**. It's a pretty little town. There's a river flowing through it – the River Conway – and an old **(2) bridge** which was built by Inigo Jones in 1636 I think. And um, it has lots of visitors in summer. The other side of this bridge is a very old **(3) cottage** that er, is very pretty. **(4) It's covered with ivy** and . . . beautiful colour in the autumn.

I: Mmm, hmm.

C: And they sell **(5) cream teas** and so the coaches come and have their **(6) scone**, **(7) jam** and **(8) cream**. And there's **(9) a putting place** on the um, the other side of the river. There used to be tennis courts there but they've done away with those. There's a nice **(10) bowling green** there. They have quite a good **(11) team** in Llanrwst. Um, and they play cricket there and they have a good cricket team as well. Lots of people go and watch it on a Saturday afternoon.

I: And is it in **(12) a valley** or up **(13) a mountain**?

C: Yes. Beautiful valley, the Conway Valley – mountains one side, quite high mountains – and **(14) fields** the other.

I: So can you see mountains from your house?

C: Oh yes, yes. Round the back of it, yes, easily. Yes, it's a very **(15) pleasant** place to live. And all the way down to the largest town which is Llandudno, **(16) a beautiful run** with trees and . . . all the way down, each side of the road.

I: And does the road follow the river down?

C: Yes, all the way down . . . to the sea, of course.

I: So Llandudno is next to the sea, then . . . or on the sea.

C: Yes. Qu . . . **(17) 'Queen of Resorts of North Wales'**, **(18) they reckon**. It is, too. It's very pretty. **(19) It hasn't been altered, hardly.** Beautiful hotels along **(20) the promenade**, and um . . .

I: Do you go there quite often?

C: Oh yes. Once a week at least, yes. Actually I do my shopping in **(21) Asda** there.

I: Oh right.

C: Take my friend and er, we have a day out on a Friday, usually.

I: So you have lunch out and . . .

C: We have. We do our shopping in Asda. **(22) Park there.** Go up town. Park there again. Have lunch in a little. . . little **(23) tiny (24) pub** called **(25) the Cottage Loaf**. And then we do the shopping at the main street, for my friend loves to shop for clothes and things. (*laughs*)

I: What time do you come home from a day in Llandudno?

C: Oh, about half-past four. We'll have gone about 10 in the morning. And my poor husband is home **(26) doing the washing**, every week, which he loves. And **(27) it's usually dry** and folded by the time I get home.

I: Does your husband do **(28) the ironing** as well?

C: No, no, no. I do that first thing on a Saturday morning. Then I go out and meet **(29) a couple of my friends** for coffee.

I: Do you go to their houses?

C: No, we meet in a little old-fashioned **(30) café** called **(31) the Hên Aelwyd**. . . . Um, only 11 till 12. Home, then, for lunch. And then whatever Saturday afternoon . . .

1 **(a) market town** – a small town in the country which is a business centre for farms and villages in the area
2 **(a) bridge** – something built over a river to allow people, vehicles or trains to cross from one side to the other
3 **(a) cottage** – a small house usually in the countryside
4 **It's covered with ivy** – Ivy is an evergreen plant which often grows up trees and buildings. Catherine has made a mistake here; in fact the plant which covers the cottage is Virginia creeper which changes from green in the summer to red in the autumn.
5 **cream teas** (plural) – A cream tea is a light meal in the afternoon where you have a pot of tea, scones, jam and cream.
6 **(a) scone** – a small, round type of cake
7 **jam** – a very thick sweet food made from boiled fruit and sugar and often eaten on toast
8 **cream** – the thick liquid which forms on the top of milk
9 **a putting place** – a small flat area of short grass where people can practise hitting golf balls into holes
10 **(a) bowling green** – a flat area of short grass where people play the game of bowls
11 **(a) team** – a group of people who do something together, for example a football team, a cricket team
12 **a valley** – an area of low land between hills or mountains often with a river running through it
13 **a mountain** – something much larger than a hill
14 **fields** (plural) – A field is a large area of land in the country where farmers grow things or where a farmer's animals feed on grass.
15 **pleasant** – nice
16 **a beautiful run** – a beautiful drive in the car
17 **'Queen of Resorts of North Wales'** – Another way of saying the best resort in North Wales. A resort is a place where people go on holiday.
18 **they reckon** – they say; this is their opinion
19 **It hasn't been altered, hardly.** – It hasn't changed very much over the years.
20 **the promenade** – a wide road next to the sea which people can walk or drive along
21 **Asda** – one of the UK's largest supermarket chains
22 **Park there.** – (We) leave the car there.
23 **tiny** – very, very small
24 **(a) pub** – a building where people go to drink alcoholic and non-alcoholic drinks, to eat and to meet friends
25 **the Cottage Loaf** – A cottage loaf is a loaf of bread which has a small round part on top of a larger round part. In this case it is the name of the pub.
26 **doing the washing** – putting the dirty clothes in the washing machine and then drying them
27 **it's usually dry and folded** – Dry is the opposite of wet. Folded means to bend the clothes so that they lie on top of each other in a pile.
28 **the ironing** – using a hot iron to make clothes flat and smooth
29 **a couple of my friends** – two or three of my friends
30 **(a) café** – a small kind of restaurant where you can buy non-alcoholic drinks and simple meals
31 **the Hên Aelwyd** – 'Hên' is a Welsh word meaning 'old' and 'Aelwyd' is a Welsh word which means the hearth or fireplace in a home where the family would sit in front of the fire and talk.

UNIT **13** Anders

A Discussion

Anders lives and works in Gothenburg in Sweden. He originally qualified as an English and German teacher, but he now works for one of Sweden's biggest training companies. He and his partner live in a new flat near a canal. Anders speaks very good English with a slight Swedish accent.

1. What do you think of when you hear the word 'Sweden'?
2. How much do you know about Sweden?

B Normalisation – gap-fill

This exercise is designed to help you get used to Anders's voice. Try to guess the missing words before you listen and discuss these with your teacher. Then listen and fill in the gaps.

1. Anders came to Gothenburg to study at the _____.
2. After his studies he got a _____ in Gothenburg.
3. He lives close to the _____.
4. Gothenburg used to be famous for _____-building.
5. Sweden experienced a financial crisis in _____.
6. The area where Anders lives was _____ for a long time.

2. Listening Comprehension

A Questions

Anders talks about the area where he lives. Listen and answer the questions.

1. Does Anders live in a house or a flat?
2. Where does he take the ferry to?
3. How long does the ferry journey from Anders's home to central Gothenburg take?
4. How long is it on foot from Anders's home to the ferry stop?

B True/false

Anders talks some more about living in Gothenburg. Answer true or false. Be prepared to give reasons for your answers.

1. _____ Anders has a fantastic view of the water from his house.
2. _____ Anders lives less than a minute from the waterfront.
3. _____ It's possible to take a ferry from central Gothenburg to Denmark and Norway.
4. _____ Anders often sees these big ferries.

C Corrections

Anders talks about Åmål, the town where he grew up. Correct the mistake in each of these sentences.

1. Åmål is about 200 miles north of Gothenburg.
2. It has around 50,000 inhabitants.
3. Anders said it was possible to cycle anywhere in Åmål.
4. There was a big fire in Åmål in the 1800s.
5. There are still lots of wooden houses in Åmål from the old days.
6. Lake Vänern is the biggest lake in Sweden.

D Gap-fill

Anders talks about his mother. Before you listen, try to predict which words, or which types of words (nouns, adjectives, prepositions, parts of verbs, etc.) will fit in the gaps. Then listen and check your answers.

1. Anders goes to _____ his mother in Åmål regularly.
2. He goes to see her in Åmål more _____ than she comes to visit him in Gothenburg.
3. This is because she's quite elderly and she finds it difficult to walk and to sit in a _____ or get on a _____ .
4. Anders and his mother often speak to each other on the _____ .

A The present simple

1. The present simple (permanent situations)

We generally use the present simple when we are talking about situations which we see as permanent. Look at these examples from the interview:

> Per-Olov said you <u>come</u> from his home town . . .
> I <u>live</u> very near to the . . . very near the water.
> the biggest ones [ships] <u>don't go</u> into town
> she <u>finds</u> it difficult to walk

To form a question in the present simple we use **do/does** + verb:

> And <u>do</u> you <u>live</u> in Gothenburg now?

2. The present simple (routines and regular actions)

We also use the present simple when we are talking about routines and things that happen regularly:

> I <u>see</u> them [the ferries] more or less every day.
> I <u>go</u> up to visit her more often than she <u>comes</u> down to Gothenburg
> We <u>talk</u> on the phone very, very often, though.

And again we use **do/does** + verb to form questions:

> <u>Do</u> you ever <u>go</u> back to Åmål?
> And <u>does</u> she ever <u>come</u> down to Gothenburg?

B The simple past

1. The simple past (regular verbs)

We use the simple past to talk about completed actions in the past, usually with reference to a time in the past. To form the simple past of regular verbs we simply add **–ed.**

The first example is when Anders talks about what happened to the land where his flat was built. After the financial crisis of 1976 it was empty for years, and then:

> all of a sudden they <u>started</u> building er, flats

The second example comes when Anders talks about growing up in Åmål. He says:

you __had__ everything you __needed__

2. The simple past (verbs ending in *-e*)

If a verb already ends in *-e*, we simply add *-d* to form the simple past:

I __moved__ away from there when I was in my 20s . . .
they __used__ to build ships in Gothenburg.

3. The simple past (irregular verbs)

There are several irregular verbs in the interview and it is a good idea to learn these. Remember, if you don't know the past tense of a verb you can just add *-ed*. Any native speaker, or competent non-native speaker, will understand your meaning.

Per-Olov __said__ you come from his home town . . .
can you tell me about where you __grew__ up
it __burnt__ down in the 1600s

C The present perfect simple with *for* and *since*

We use the present perfect simple to talk about things which have (or haven't) happened during a period of time leading up to the present. To form the present perfect simple we use the verb *have* + past participle. We often use the present perfect simple with *for* and *since*. Look at these examples:

1. The present perfect simple with *for*:

'I __have lived__ here __for__ nine years.'
'He __hasn't seen__ her __for__ weeks.'
'He __hasn't had__ anything to eat __for__ hours.'
'We __have had__ no rain __for__ days.'

2. The present perfect simple with *since*:

'I __have lived__ here __since__ 2001.'
'I __have been__ here __since__ two o'clock.'

'He <u>hasn't eaten</u> anything <u>since</u> breakfast.'

'We <u>have had</u> brilliant weather <u>since</u> May.'

Now look at this example of the present perfect simple with *since* taken from the interview:

I live in Gothenburg now and I've lived there ever since I started university . . .

4. Further Listening Practice

A Recognising individual words in a stream of speech – dictation

 to

Work with a partner. Listen to the excerpts from Anders's interview and write them down. Then check your answers with another pair.

1. _____.

2. _____.

3. _____?

4. _____.

5. _____.

6. _____.

Gothenburg

B Hearing the sounds of English 1

Listen and repeat each minimal pair after the speaker.

his/is	live/leave
right/light	had/hat
think/sink	

C Discriminating between minimal pairs of sounds 1

Tick (✓) the boxes which correspond to the words you hear.

1	1	2	3	4	5
his					
is					
2	1	2	3	4	5
right					
light					
3	1	2	3	4	5
think					
sink					
4	1	2	3	4	5
live					
leave					
5	1	2	3	4	5
had					
hat					

D Contractions

Contractions are common in informal spoken and written English, such as two friends chatting, emails between friends, and so on, but not in more formal English such as lectures, speeches and letters to companies.

Look at the following excerpts from the interview and put in the contracted forms of the underlined words. Then listen to find out if you were correct.

Example: Yes, <u>that is</u> right. **that's**

1. and <u>I have lived</u> there ever since I started university . . . _____

2. <u>It is</u> about four or five minutes, so you <u>cannot</u> complain.
    _____ / _____

3. <u>That is</u> quite nice. _____
4. the biggest ones <u>do not</u> go into town _____
5. <u>they are</u> too big _____
6. So you said <u>it is</u> 200 kilometres north of Gothenburg. _____
7. Yeah. <u>That is</u> the second-biggest er, lake in Sweden. _____
8. <u>That is</u> a bit confusing. _____
9. <u>I have</u> still got my mother up there . . . _____
10. <u>she is</u> quite old. _____

E Hearing the sounds of English 2

As with Exercise B, listen and repeat each minimal pair after the speaker.

years/jeers	back/pack
north/Norse	grew/glue
old/hold	

F Discriminating between minimal pairs of sounds 2

Tick (✓) the boxes which correspond to the words you hear.

1	1	2	3	4	5
years					
jeers					
2	1	2	3	4	5
north					
Norse					
3	1	2	3	4	5
old					
hold					
4	1	2	3	4	5
back					
pack					
5	1	2	3	4	5
grew					
glue					

G Simplification – weak forms

As we heard with both Danny and Catherine, when we speak quickly a process known as 'simplification' occurs. Basically the speaker takes short cuts and doesn't articulate unstressed words fully. The term 'weak forms' refers to very common grammatical words such as prepositions whose pronunciation changes significantly in fast, informal spoken English. Some of the most common weak forms are *of*, *for*, *from* and *to*.

First predict which words fit in the gaps, then listen to check your answers.

1. the western part _____ Sweden
2. but I moved away _____ there when I was in my 20s
3. I moved _____ Gothenburg.
4. the area was empty _____ years and years
5. and then all _____ a sudden they started building er, flats
6. you can actually take the ferry _____ work
7. nothing _____ that kind

How does the pronunciation of *to*, *for*, *from* and *of* change in informal spoken English?

H Hearing the sounds of English 3

As with Exercises B and E, listen and repeat each minimal pair after the speaker.

lake/rake	said/set
still/steel	all/hall
but/putt	

I Discriminating between minimal pairs of sounds 3

Tick (✓) the boxes which correspond to the words you hear.

1	1	2	3	4	5
lake					
rake					
2	1	2	3	4	5
still					
steel					
3	1	2	3	4	5
but					
putt					
4	1	2	3	4	5
said					
set					
5	1	2	3	4	5
all					
hall					

J Simplification – elision

As we heard with Danny and Catherine, when we speak quickly a process known as elision occurs – this is the missing out of sounds, particularly *–d* and *–t*. Elision makes it difficult for you to recognise even those words that are part of your active vocabulary.

Fill in the missing words in the following extracts from the interview, all of which have been affected by elision.

1. when I _____ _____ start my studies
2. I _____ _____ Gothenburg . . .
3. I've _____ _____ ever since I started university . . .
4. it's _____ _____ minutes
5. you _____ _____
6. the biggest ones _____ _____ into town
7. Yeah. That's the _____-_____ er, lake in Sweden.
8. That's a _____ _____.
9. Do you ever go _____ _____ Åmål?

A **Extension exercise**   Fill in the blanks in these new sentences with words you heard during Anders's interview.

> build   burnt   complain   confusing
> empty   ferry   home   lake   left   moved
> since   toes   too   used   water

1. I'm going _____ — I'm really tired.

2. That park over there is where I _____ to play football when I was a kid.

3. We _____ here two years ago because we wanted a home with a garden.

4. I'm starving! I haven't had anything to eat _____ breakfast.

5. I love swimming, but I hate going under the _____.

6. The Government is going to _____ another 100,000 homes for the needy over the next five years.

7. I need to get some more petrol — the tank's nearly _____.

8. We started off in Athens and then we took a _____ to a nearby island.

9. I know it rained yesterday, but the weather's been wonderful for the past month or so, so we can't _____.

10. The instructor began the lesson by telling us to bend over and touch our _____.

11. We had the picnic under a tree because it was _____ hot to sit in the sun.

12. I'm sorry — I've _____ the toast again.

13. Is there any mashed potato _____? I'm really hungry.

14. At the top of the mountain there's a _____ where you can go swimming or sailing in summer.

15. The road signs were a bit _____ so I got lost twice, but I was only 20 minutes late.

B Verbs in the simple past

Change the verb stem in each bracket into the simple past. All the verbs are taken from the interview and appeared in the simple past.

1. We (move) _____ here in 2005.

2. When I was young I (want) _____ to be a train driver when I (grow) _____ up.

3. I (stop) _____ eating meat when I (be) _____ 17.

4. I (have) _____ to stay late at work yesterday because I (need) _____ to finish a report.

5. When I (be) _____ young I (can) _____ cycle up this hill without stopping!

6. Where's Peter got to? He (say) _____ he would be here at eight.

C Prepositions and adverbs

Put the correct preposition or adverb in the gaps. They are all taken from the interview. Some of them are used more than once.

> about   at   away   back   down   far   for   from
> in   into   near   of   on   since   to   up   with

1. Where do you come _____?

2. We live _____ north-east London.

3. I haven't seen you _____ ages.

4. Would you like some milk _____ your tea?

5. Can you get your dog _____ from the food, please?

6. I've been waiting for a bus _____ six o'clock.

7. Come round to my place tonight and tell me all _____ your holiday.

8. It's a beautiful house, but it's very _____ a main road, so there's always a lot _____ traffic noise, even _____ night.

9. How _____ is it from your house _____ the town centre?

10. I was walking along the street on my way to work when suddenly I walked_____ a lamp-post.

11. I can see Notre Dame Cathedral _____ my office window!

12. Someone stood _____ my toe on the subway and now it's black and blue.

13. I walked _____ and _____ the market for hours yesterday looking for strawberries.

14. Brighton is about 60 miles south _____ London _____ the south coast.

15. This garden reminds me _____ the one my grandmother had when I was growing _____.

16. I need to go _____ home. I think I left the window open.

17. My son's always _____ his mobile phone these days.

I: OK. Now um, Per-Olov said you come from his home town, which is Åmål, I think?

A: Yes, that's right. Er, I used to live there for 20 years and er, Åmål, that's a small little town er, in the western part of Sweden, with some 15 . . . 10 to 15,000 **(1) inhabitants.** Er, but I moved away from there when I was in my 20s when I had to . . . or when I wanted to start my studies, so I, I've . . . I moved to Gothenburg.

I: Right. And do you live in Gothenburg now?

A: I live in Gothenburg now and I've lived there ever since I started university and I got a job.

I: Right. OK. Um, so tell me about where you live in Gothenburg.

A: Er, I live very near to the . . . very near the water. Er, there have . . . they, they, they used to build ships in Gothenburg. It was very big until 1976 when everything was sort of stopped during **(2) the crisis** we had back then. And er, the area was empty for years and years and then **(3) all of a sudden** they started building er, flats, and er, luckily enough I, I live in one of those over there, so the area is new, er, the flat is new and er, you can actually take **(4) the ferry** to work.

I: Really?

A: Which is quite nice!

I: (*laughs*) How far is it to get the ferry from where you live?

A: Er, it's about 20 minutes . . .

I: OK.

A: . . . from where I live into the central parts of Gothenburg.

I: OK. And do you have to walk long to **(5) the ferry stop?**

A: Er, not very long. It's about four or five minutes, so you can't complain.

I: Do you get . . . well, can you see the water from where you live?

A: Er, well, if I stand on my **(6) toes** I can . . .

I: Right.

A: . . . but er, it only takes . . . well, 30 seconds to reach the, the waterfront and um, that's quite nice.

I: Mmm. OK. Um, do you get ships going up and down **(7) the canal?**

A: Oh yes, er, the biggest ones don't go into town because . . . well, they're, they're too big, but er, we have the, the ferries going to Denmark and Germany and er, they go right into the centre of town, so I see them more or less every day.

I: Really?

A: That's quite nice.

I: Ah, brilliant.

I: OK. Um, can you tell me about where you grew up, which was Åmål, I think.

A: Yes, Åmål, that is about 200 kilometres north of Gothenburg. Er, **(8) a small, industrial town** with . . . well, 10 to 15,000 inhabitants. Er, it was really a **(9) calm,** nice, little . . . little town with er, well, all your friends, all your families – everybody was there and er, you had everything you needed and everything was er . . . I mean, you could walk anywhere.

I: Right.

A: No buses, no . . . nothing of that kind.

I: You said it was industrial. Was it a pretty town, or?

A: It is a really, really pretty town. Er, it was a wooden town but it burnt down in the 1600s and er, they had to rebuild all of it. So there are a, a few houses still left **(10) that reminds you of what it used to be like,** but er . . . yes, it's a, it's a really, really pretty town.

I: So you said it's 200 kilometres north of Gothenburg. Is it by the sea?

A: Er, yes. It's by er, the Väner, Väner Lake.

I: Oh, **(11) a lake.**

A: Yeah. That's the second-biggest er, lake in Sweden.

I: Mhm, hmm. So when you say 'sea', that . . . does that mean 'lake'?

A: That's means ja, it's a, it's a . . . ja, it means lake.

I: **(12) That's a bit confusing.**

A: It is. It certainly is.

I: Hmm. Do you ever go back to Åmål?

A: Yes. I've still got my mother up there, so I visit her regularly. Not as often as she wants, though, but er . . . I, I try to as often as I can.

I: Right. And does she ever come down to Gothenburg?

A: It happens, so . . . well, I go, I go up to visit her more often than she comes down to Gothenburg because er, she's quite old and she finds it difficult to walk and er, to sit in a car or to get onto a train or something. But er . . . we see each other. We talk on the phone very, very often, though.

I: OK. That's nice.

1   inhabitants (plural) **an inhabitant**– An inhabitant is someone who lives in a particular place.
2   **the crisis** – a time of suffering or uncertainty (in this case a financial crisis)
3   **all of a sudden** – very quickly
4   **the ferry** – a boat or ship taking passengers to and from places as a regular service
5   **the ferry stop** – the place where passengers get on or off a ferry
6   toes (plural) **a toe** – A toe is one of the the five separate points at the end of your feet (equivalent to the fingers on your hand).
7   **the canal** – a man-made channel for water
8   **a small, industrial town** – a small town where products are made in factories
9   **calm** – quiet, peaceful
10 **that reminds you of what it used to be like** – that gives you an idea of how it used to be
11 **a lake** – a large area of water surrounded by land
12 **That's a bit confusing.** – That's a little bit difficult to understand.

UNIT **14** Jackie

Normalisation

We heard Jackie talking about her family in Unit 1. Jackie comes from Cardiff in South Wales, but she now lives in Cornwall in south-west England. Her accent is a mix of South Welsh and Cornish.

This exercise is designed to help you get used to Jackie's voice. Listen to the interview and write down as many words as you can.

Gap-fill

Jackie talks about her local area in Cornwall, in south-west England. Before you listen, try to predict which words, or which types of words (nouns, adjectives, prepositions, parts of verbs, etc.) will fit in the gaps. Then listen and check your answers.

1. Carlyon Bay is right on the _____.
2. Jackie and her husband live up the _____ from a small _____.
3. There is a beautiful _____ below them.
4. It's called _____ Harbour.
5. They keep _____ ships down in the harbour.
6. These are very old ships which they use when they make _____.
7. They filmed Mansfield _____ near where Jackie lives, and the last_____Musketeers film.
8. Near the harbour there is also a _____.
9. There are beautiful _____ beaches all around Carlyon Bay.
10. Jackie says the whole area is wonderful, but very _____.
11. A lot of people come to Cornwall on _____.

A **Extension exercise**   Fill in the blanks in these new sentences with words you heard during Jackie's interview.

> beaches   been   fields   harbour   last
> like   make   tell   village   well   world

1.   I've never _____ to Sweden. What's it _____?

2.   Come and _____ me what you did at school today.

3.   I grew up in a little _____ in the country, but I moved to London when I was 20.

4.   The place we were staying in was right next to a _____ full of little fishing boats.

5.   I think they should _____ a film about your life. You've done so many interesting things.

6.   I prefer sandy _____ to ones with stones.

7.   There are lots of sheep in the _____ behind our house.

8.   My favourite city in the _____ is Munich.

9.   That's the _____ time I lend you any money!

10. Shall we invite Anders as _____?

B Prepositions and adverbs

Put the correct preposition or adverb in the gaps. They are all taken from the interview. One of them is used twice.

> around   down   for   from   in
> like   of   on   over   to

1. Which US state is Boston _____? Is it Massachusetts?
2. We're going on holiday _____ Switzerland next week.
3. We've got a little holiday cottage _____ the west coast of Scotland.
4. This is the best knife _____ peeling potatoes.
5. When I have a day off I love walking _____ the shops.
6. We're just been _____ that new Mexican restaurant. It was brilliant!
7. What's your new manager _____? Do you get on with her?
8. We live about five minutes _____ the train station, so we can pick you up if you like.
9. My best friend lives _____ the road, so we see a lot _____ each other.
10. My cousin has travelled all _____ the world.

Cornwall

I: You live in **(1) Carlyon Bay**, I think, in **(2) Cornwall**.

J: Yes.

I: I've, I've never been to that **(3) area**. Can you tell me what it's like? Can you describe it to me?

J: It's right on the coast. Um . . .

I: Where, where you live is right on the coast?

J: Where, where I live, yes. **(4) We actually um, live up the fields from a small village on the coast.** There's a beautiful harbour down there. And er . . .

I: What's that called?

J: It's Charlestown Harbour. And er, they actually keep er,

(5) tall ships down there. There . . . these very old masted ships that they use er, they, they use them all over the world for, for making . . . in . . . when they make films. And er, they were used . . . last time they filmed down here they've, they've done **(6) Mansfield Park** and er, the last **(7) Three Musketeers** film was, was made down here. They do a lot of filming around Cornwall. And there's a nice . . . there's a harbour and a beach, and we have other beaches as well, beautiful sandy beaches. And we have **(8) the Eden Project**. And the, the whole area is, is wonderful. It's, it's er, very touristy, a lot of, lot of people come on holiday down here.

5. Words and Phrases

1   **Carlyon Bay** – The name of the bay is Carlyon. A bay is part of the coast where the land curves in a semi-circle.

2   **Cornwall** – the most south-westerly county in England

3   **(an) area** – a particular part of the country

4   **We actually, live up the fields from a small village on the coast.** – Jackie is being more exact here. She doesn't really live right next to the sea, but she does live very close to it. The village is on the coast, then there are some fields and then there's Jackie's house.

5   **tall ships** – old ships with huge masts (A mast is the tall pole on a ship which supports the sails.)

6   **Mansfield Park** – a film based on the famous book of that title by Jane Austen

7   **(The) Three Musketeers** – three characters created by Alexandre Dumas in his books

8   **the Eden Project** – a popular tourist attraction in Cornwall consisting of two enormous domes (i.e. giant greenhouses) where you can see plants and trees from all over the world

UNIT **15** Tammy

We heard Tammy talking about her family in Unit 3. Tammy grew up in Canada but left in her 20s. She now works as a theatre sister and lives in east London, but she has retained her Canadian accent.

Normalisation

This exercise is designed to help you get used to Tammy's voice. Before you listen, try to predict which words, or which types of words (nouns, adjectives, prepositions, parts of verbs, etc.) will fit in the gaps. Then listen and check your answers.

1. Chilliwack is a very small _____ outside Vancouver.
2. It's surrounded by _____, _____ and lakes.
3. It's a very pretty _____ community.
4. Chilliwack is about _____ miles from Vancouver.

2. Listening Comprehension

Gap-fill

Before you listen, try to predict which words, or which types of words will fit in the gaps. Then listen and check your answers.

1. Tammy says Vancouver is a really pretty _____.
2. It's surrounded by _____.
3. It overlooks the _____ and the bay.
4. The University of _____ Columbia is on a peninsula.
5. English Bay is where all the _____ wait to come into the _____.
6. Vancouver has some beautiful _____.
7. The Lion's Gate Bridge begins in Stanley _____.
8. This is in the _____ of Vancouver.
9. The Lion's Gate Bridge ends on the _____ Shore.
10. All the _____ people live there in their big, fancy _____.
11. There are two ski _____ in Vancouver: The Cypress Bowl and Grouse Mountain.
12. They have _____ skiing there all _____.
13. The oldest part of Vancouver is called _____.
14. The oldest _____ in Vancouver is about _____ years old.

3. Further Language Development

A Extension exercise

Fill in the blanks in these new sentences with words you heard during Tammy's interview.

> called   grew   heart   outside   park
> rich   small   wait   winter

1. What's your cat _____?

2. Shall I wait _____ in the car?

3. My father _____ up in Southampton, but he moved to Bristol when he was 18.

4. Could I just have a _____ piece of cake, please? I'm not very hungry.

5. Can you _____ for me? I just need to change my shoes.

6. There's a little _____ near us where the kids play football on Saturdays.

7. You know what they say — cold hands, warm _____!

8. They're not _____, but they have enough money to live comfortably.

9. We had loads of snow last _____.

B Prepositions and adverbs

Put the correct preposition or adverb in the gaps. They are all taken from the interview. Some of them are used twice.

> across   as   at   by   from   in   of   up

1. I think children grow _____ too quickly these days.
2. They live in a little village surrounded _____ hills.
3. Why don't you come _____ out of the cold?
4. How long does it take you to get home _____ work?
5. She's got a wonderful apartment _____ the centre of Washington DC.
6. If you stand in our kitchen you get a beautiful view _____ to the other side of the valley.
7. Do you get lots _____ rain here in winter?
8. This restaurant is just _____ nice as the Peking Chef and it's half _____ expensive.
9. I left Martin _____ home because he isn't feeling _____ all well.

Vancouver

Part 1   (18")

I: Um, where in Canada did you grow up?

T: I grew up in a place called Chilliwack – a very small town outside of Vancouver, **(1) surrounded by mountains**, rivers and lakes. Very pretty. Farming community.

I: Right. Er, how close was it to Vancouver?

T: About 65 miles.

Part 2   (1'27")

I: Can you tell me about Vancouver?

T: It's a really pretty city. It's surrounded by mountains. **(2) It's overlooking the ocean** and **(3) the bay**. Er, the University of British Columbia is actually on **(4) a peninsula** that overlooks the ocean. And then there's a place called English Bay, which is where all the ships wait to come in to the harbour. Um, they've got some beautiful, beautiful bridges. The er, Lion's Gate Bridge which takes you from Stanley Park, which is a large park **(5) in the heart of** Vancouver across to **(6) the North Shore**, which is where all the rich people live **(7) in their big, fancy houses**. Um, there's two ski hills in Vancouver, one Cypress Bowl and one called Grouse Mountain and they have night skiing there all winter. And they, I think they do man-made snow and so on, but it's, it's there. Um, it's just a really pretty city. It's got lots of **(8) arts and crafts** and things to do and see.

I: Is it um, very old?

T: Er, not as old as er, you'd think. It's not very old at all. It . . . I would say hundred and something. It's not very old at all.

I: Does, does it have an old part of the town?

T: Um, it's got a place called Gastown, which has now become a very touristy area. And that was the original . . . one of the original places. The oldest hotel in there is Hotel Vancouver and that's only about 60, 70, no, 70? About 70 years old, so it's not that old itself, so that's the one that was built first, so . . .

5. Words and Phrases

1   **surrounded by mountains** – there are mountains all around it

2   **It's overlooking the ocean** – from the city you get a good view of the ocean

3   **the bay** – A bay is part of the coast where the land curves in a semi-circle.

4   **a peninsula** – a long piece of land which sticks out into the ocean

5   **in the heart of Vancouver** – in the centre of Vancouver

6   **the North Shore** – A shore is land at the edge of an ocean, lake or wide river.

7   **in their big, fancy houses** – in their large, expensive houses

8   **arts and crafts** – things made by hand

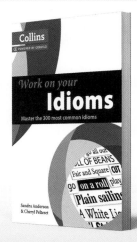

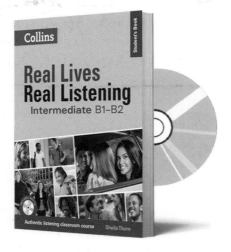
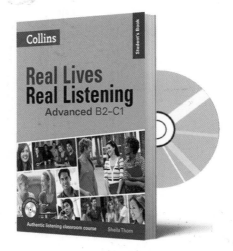 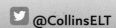